TIME
MANAGEMENT
== *for the* ==
CHRISTIAN
LEADER

TIME MANAGEMENT
for the
CHRISTIAN
LEADER

· · · · · · · · · · · · · · · ·

Or
HOW TO
SQUEEZE BLOOD
FROM A TURNIP

KEN WILLARD
Foreword by
Mike Schreiner

Abingdon Press
Nashville

TIME MANAGEMENT FOR THE CHRISTIAN LEADER:
OR HOW TO SQUEEZE BLOOD FROM A TURNIP

Copyright © 2015 by Ken Willard

This book is printed on acid-free paper.

Library of Congress Cataloging-in-Publication Data has been requested.

ISBN: 978-1-63088-425-3

15 16 17 18 19 20 21 22 23 24—10 9 8 7 6 5 4 3 2 1
MANUFACTURED IN THE UNITED STATES OF AMERICA

CONTENTS

If I only had an hour to chop down a tree, I would spend the first forty-five minutes sharpening my axe.

—Abraham Lincoln

FOREWORD

Twice a year, compliments of daylight saving time, most of us experience the gain or loss of one solitary hour of time. Sixty precious minutes. In spring, we "spring" forward and lose an hour of sleep but gain an hour of sunlight in the evening. In fall, our clocks get reset as we "fall" back, gaining an hour of sleep but getting less daylight in the evening. While "time keeps on slippin', into the future," as the song "Fly Like an Eagle" by The Steve Miller Band says, we have different ways of marking time. And not just with daylight saving time.

As Christians, we mark time differently than the rest of the world. We live in two "time zones" simultaneously. One is called *chronos* time. *Chronos* time is what we measure with our calendars and watches. It's divided into neat, orderly, and well-defined segments—years, months, weeks, and days; hours, minutes, and seconds.

But we also live in another time zone. *Kairos* time. In the New Testament, *kairos* is the appointed time in the purpose of God. It is the time when God acts. In those transcendent moments, we experience the in-breaking of God—the coming of God's kingdom from up there in heaven to down here on earth, those things that cause us to pause and recognize God is with us.

If you are like me, you often find yourself so immersed in, and driven by, *chronos* time that it is challenging to sense and experience the *kairos*. Yet God is present all around us, all day long. The Holy Spirit whispers to us as we drive our kids to school in the morning: "Let go of any frustrations you experienced packing lunches this morning, and make sure your daughter's emotional backpack is filled before you drop her off." God's word echoes in our minds as we work our way through our e-mail inboxes and our daily duties; it is prompting us to draw on eternal truth. Jesus nudges us as we notice the teenager sitting alone on the park bench with his head buried in his hands. God is present at all times and in all places. Are you noticing?

God with us makes all the difference. Divine presence can transform a routine day of meeting clients into a series of divine appointments. Awareness of God with us can reframe something mundane, like checking off the weekly list of household chores, into a sacramental moment of grace.

So the challenge before us is two-fold. First, in all we do, to be fully present with God and those right in front of us, which allows us to, second, make the most of every opportunity in which God has placed us.

Life—and thus, time, itself—is a gift from God. Contrary to the language we use, we can't *make* time or *take* time. That's God's business. He is the creator. We are stewards. We receive what God has entrusted to us, and we invest it as wisely as possible. So, as Christian leaders, how we steward and manage our time matters.

Time Management for the Christian Leader is a must-read for every Christian leader. In this concise book, my friend Ken Willard, has distilled several decades of leadership and learning into an invaluable resource. After spending the first half of his life helping Fortune 500 companies maximize their *chronos* time, Ken has heeded the call of God to help those of us immersed in the *kairos* world.

What I want you to know is that Ken is the genuine article. He speaks truth from his experience. Fifteen years ago, he earned my invitation to be the first chairperson of our new church's administrative board. How? He was willing to show up every week at our rented facilities two hours before services started to clean windows and bathrooms; vacuum floors; and invest his time, talent, and treasure in the things of God. That was just the beginning of how God began to call him to leverage his one and only life for kingdom/*kairos* purposes.

In the years that have followed, Ken has helped ministry leaders across the country get a better handle on their time. He's helped me realize the necessity of investing time to plan, which has benefited my entire organization. Our church staff and leaders are less frustrated with last-minute tasks. And in turn, we have all become more fruitful in our calling to equip God's people and expand God's kingdom.

To make the most of this one and only life we've been entrusted with from God, I invite you to remember that God has a plan and purpose for us being present in creation at this precise moment in human history. You and me. Right here. Right now. As Jesus announced, "The kingdom of heaven has come near" (Matt 10:7).

As Christian leaders, we can't let time *fly* and *pass us by.* There is simply too much at stake. Instead, we must follow the lead of King David, who "served God's purpose in his own generation" (Acts 13:36). And then we will surely receive the words God destined us to hear: "Excellent! You are a good and faithful servant.... Come, celebrate with me" (Matt 25:21).

Rev. Mike Schreiner
Lead Pastor, Morning Star Church

INTRODUCTION

Tired of trying to get blood from a turnip?

In 2008, I found myself in a tough place. The company where I was employed laid off all of the field human resource people due to the downturn in the economy. My training team and I were included. Three months prior to that, my wife and I had lost our only child, Amanda Leigh, in a car accident. She was on her way home from college for her twentieth birthday the next day. With no good prospects for employment, I decided to start my own consulting company with plans to partner with small- to medium-size organizations to help them in various areas of leadership training and development. God had other plans.

With the help of many good friends and fellow trainers, I wrote a small time management book called, *Time Management for Peak Performance: Practical Plans for Practical People*. My plans at the time were to use the book mainly as a marketing piece to help get my foot in the door with a company. I received a loan from my father and had 250 copies of the book printed through a self-publishing company. Over the years, I sold about a thousand copies from my basement office: mostly to pastors, churches, and church leaders going through one of the church leadership programs I created.

My pastor, Mike Schreiner at Morning Star Church, called me one day to help him with a peer mentoring class he was leading. The topic that session focused on coaching church staff or leaders to improve their behavior/performance, and Mike knew that I had done some work in this area with a couple of businesses. While we were there that day, Mike introduced me to Bob Farr, Director of Congregational Excellence for the Missouri Annual Conference of the United Methodist Church, and Dr. David P. Hyatt, a pastor who is now a church consultant and coach. I'll cut to the chase here... they hired me to create pastoral and laity leadership development curriculum for the whole conference. (Which have since been used in over a dozen other conferences.) One of the sessions they wanted was on time management, and we ended up using my book.

Even though my plans were to work in the business world, the only door that opened for me was in the church. Thanks to the wisdom and leadership of others, I have been able to work full-time in God's kingdom ever since. During this time, many pastors and church leaders purchased my time management book, and I pray that it helped them develop that area of their leadership gift.

So why write a new time management book? There are several key reasons I feel moved at this time to write this book: First, there is a need to speak more to my audience and meet them where they are on their leadership journey. The vast majority of those whom I work with in this area or who have bought my first book are Christian leaders, pastors, or lay leaders. I feel compelled to put time management in terms that are consistent with who they are and the environment in which they work and serve. Second, this is one of the top requested leadership topics I encounter as I coach pastors, work with church staffs, or facilitate leadership workshops. As such, there are many areas of time management that have come up during the past few years that I did not address in my other book. Finally, and I think most importantly, I'm learning to listen more than I speak, and the voice of the Holy Spirit is leading me to write this now.

This book will borrow heavily from my previous one. I am going to cover all the same areas of time management but in a new way and, of course, with a very intentional focus on us as Christian leaders. I'm still going to share some of my favorite quotes on the subject, but I am also going to have scripture verses that relate to our topic.

Do you feel like you're trying to squeeze blood from a turnip when it comes to your time management skills? As I'm sure you know already, you cannot get blood from a turnip. And I hate to disappoint you so soon into the book, but I cannot give you any more time each day, week, month, or year. However, my prayer and my strong belief is that you will find several ways contained within these pages to better manage your time.

God gives each of us 168 hours to use each week. Why is it that some of us seem to spend our time more effectively and more efficiently than others? If you are reading this book then you have a desire to grow your gift of leadership in the area of time management. I celebrate that step on your journey.

There is a quote from Warren G. Bennis that many of us have heard over the years: "Managers do things right. Leaders do the right things" (Bennis, *Leaders*). While I certainly think that is true. I would add that Christian leaders do the right thing for God's kingdom, and not just for themselves.

Throughout my career in business and as a leader in my local church, I have been a student of time management. Initially, it was just as a way to improve myself, and then I began teaching workshops on time management with several different organizations. Looking back, that was all in preparation for working with church leaders. This book will incorporate much of what I have read, taught, and learned over the course of my career.

The goal of this book is not to be the sum of all time management information available. That would take too many pages and take too much time to read. (Sort of defeats the purpose of time management to write a book so big no one has the time to read it.) My goal is to present what I consider the most important and practical information for us as Christian leaders. My prayer is that you find at least one thing somewhere in this book that you will be able to apply in your ministry.

On second thought—maybe we can get some blood out of that turnip!

ON SECOND THOUGHT—MAYBE WE CAN GET SOME BLOOD OUT OF THAT TURNIP!

In fact, throughout the book you will hear from leaders who have been doing just that. In a section I am calling "Squeezing the Turnip," you will find some words of wisdom from leaders who are practicing many of the concepts we will cover. These should be good words of encouragement as you focus on improving your own time management skills.

Let's go into this journey with the expectation of learning something new, hearing something old in a new way, and growing ourselves as leaders in God's kingdom.

Planning is bringing the future into the present so you
can do something about it now.

—Alan Lakein

HOW TO USE THIS BOOK

The plans of the diligent lead to profit as surely as haste leads to poverty.

—Proverbs 21:5

The best way to get the most out of this book is to read through it "actively" by making notes, filling in the blanks, and answering the questions as you go. Focus on getting something you can apply right away from each section. You will find "Coaching Corners" in each chapter to help you process what we have covered and to keep everything connected. These are coaching questions that I might ask you related to the topic if we were having a coaching session. I also include a section at the end of each chapter for discussion questions if you are using this resource in a Sunday school class, small group, leadership team, administrative board, or just to help you go a little deeper.

While many people will read through this book in one sitting or at least without pausing much between the chapters, that is not my intent. I would encourage you to not rush through the book too fast. The concepts we are going to cover are big and depending on where you are now in your ability to manage your time, there is likely too much for you to try and absorb in one sitting.

I WOULD ENCOURAGE YOU TO NOT RUSH THROUGH THE BOOK TOO FAST.

Here are a few ideas about how you might best use this book:

1. Schedule a day away—A personal retreat away from everything and everyone else. Grab your Bible, a note pad, and this book and get away for eight hours or so. Read a chapter, reflect and pray about what spoke to you, and make some notes about what you are going to go back and do next.

2. Go through the book a chapter at a time with your Sunday school class, small group, ministry, or leadership team. Ensure you have at least a week between each session for everyone to process what is being covered.

3. Read a chapter every week or two, and then have a coaching session to process what was covered. A professional coach can help you take appropriate steps and hold you accountable to your commitments.

When I coach pastors and laity leaders I explain to them that my goal is to meet them where they are on their leadership journey and to help them take the next step. Be careful as you read through these pages that you do not try to bite off too much at one time. It will only cause you more frustration instead of helping you manage your time. Stay focused on that next step God is calling you to take. So grab a pen, a highlighter, and your Bible so we can discover how we can all make the most of the time God has given us today!

TIME
MANAGEMENT
== *for the* ==
CHRISTIAN
LEADER

What Is Time?

According to the Merriam-Webster online dictionary:

> *Time: (noun) the measured or measurable period during which an action, process, or condition exists or continues.*

In our world:

> *. . . it's a resource, a resource that must be managed.*

> —Al Lucia and Donna Long, *JukeBox Journey to Success*

According to God:

> *Let me know my end, LORD.*
> *How many days do I have left?*
> *I want to know how brief my time is."*
> *You've made my days so short;*
> *my lifetime is like nothing in your eyes.*
> *Yes, a human life is nothing but a puff of air!*
> *Yes, people wander around like shadows;*
> *yes, they hustle and bustle, but pointlessly;*
> *they don't even know who will get the wealth they've amassed.*

> —Psalm 39: 4-6

Chapter 1

THE JOURNEY

Where are we going?

The priest replied to them, "Go in peace. The LORD is watching over you on this trip you've taken."

—Judges 18:6

It's all about you.

In 2002, Pastor Rick Warren wrote a very popular book called, *The Purpose Driven Life* that starts with the sentence, "It's not about you." While that is certainly true in the big picture, when we focus on the "why" component of managing our time God has given us, we do need to start with a little self-reflection.

> ## Coaching Corner
> What do you really, really want?
>
> Why is that important to you?

When I look at a map of the exodus route the Israelites took from Egypt, the first thing that comes to mind is, "too bad no one had a GPS." Do you ever get the feeling you are wandering in the wilderness? The first phase of time management we are going to look at focuses on purpose.

- Why is it important for you to get the most from your time?

- What specific area of time management do you struggle with the most?

- Where would you like to spend more of your time if it were possible?

Only you can answer these questions. Is it important for you to maximize your time so you can spend more time with your family? With God? With your community? Are you struggling to keep up with all your commitments at work? Maybe you have reached the point in your career where you are tired of putting in over seventy hours a week and always feeling like you never get enough done. Whatever the reason, the true purpose of time management must be clear to you and important enough for you to realize that something must change.

One of my favorite quotes is often attributed to Albert Einstein: "Insanity: doing the same thing over and over again and expecting different results." The truth is that for us to get different results in our time management, we will have to change some behaviors. The rest of this book will give you some ideas and suggestions for how to do this, but it must start with you. So I ask again, why is it important for you to get the most from your time?

THE TRUTH IS THAT FOR US TO GET DIFFERENT RESULTS IN OUR TIME MANAGEMENT, WE WILL HAVE TO CHANGE SOME BEHAVIORS.

This purpose will become the catalyst for everything that follows. When you encounter struggles along the way, and I guarantee that you will, this purpose is what will enable you to get back on track.

In 1984, I was going to school at a local community college and decided to take a semester off to get married. That semester turned quickly into about twenty years. While I had always wanted to get a college degree, working full-time to support my family was more important, and I never could figure out a way to go back to school.

As our daughter got older and started looking at where to attend a college, the desire for my own degree became stronger. The ability to take classes online on my own schedule as I traveled also made this possible for the first time. The *purpose* of attaining a college degree changed from just something that I always wanted to do into a passion to match what our daughter was doing. It was that purpose that kept me going though many challenging days and courses.

Take a minute right now and read your life verse. If you do not have one particular Bible verse already identified, then look through the books of Proverbs, Psalms, Matthew, Mark, Luke, John, and Acts until you find a verse that really jumps out at you. Then prayerfully and truthfully answer the questions on the Discussion Questions page. Do not worry about writing your responses out perfectly or even in complete sentences. This is only for you. Share with others only if you feel compelled to do so.

The key is that you understand why it is important for you to improve your time management skills at this time.

Now let's see how we can take that foundation of *purpose* and start building on it to ultimately reach our goals of increased productivity and more time for the areas which are most important to us.

Having a purpose is the difference between making a living and making a life.

—Tom Thiss

Chapter 1

What Would You Do with an Extra Hour Every Day?

The Huffington Post conducted a survey of 1,000 adults and asked them what they would do with an extra hour. Here are the top five responses:

36%—Relax

27%—Sleep

27%—Spend time with family or friends

24%—Athletic activity/exercise

20%—Housework

"Only thirteen percent of respondents said they have enough time to accomplish the things that are important every day—a feeling so prevalent that researchers have taken to calling it 'time famine'" (Belkin, "HuffPost Poll").

Discussion Questions

Why is it important for you personally to get the most from your time?

What specific area of time management do you struggle with the most? Where are you challenged?

What areas of time management do you feel are currently strengths? What are you doing well that you'd like to grow?

Where would you like to spend more of your time if it were possible?
- ❏ Family and friends
- ❏ Reading and reflecting on scripture
- ❏ Prayer—talking and listening to God
- ❏ Exercise and athletic activities
- ❏ Sleeping
- ❏ Relaxing
- ❏ Housework
- ❏ Home repairs
- ❏ Serving in the community
- ❏ Work
- ❏ Watching television
- ❏ Serving at church
- ❏ Something else

_____

_____

_____

The truth is, we cannot manage the clock.... managing time is really about managing, even orchestrating, the occurrence of activities in our lives.

—Warren "Trapper" Woods, CSP and William A. Guillory, PhD, *Tick Tock! Who Broke the Clock?*

Plans fail with no counsel, but with many counselors they succeed.

—Proverbs 15:22

Teach us to number our days so we can have a wise heart.

—Psalm 90:12

Chapter 2

STRATEGIC PLANNING

What is most important to you... and to God?

My plans aren't your plans, nor are your ways my ways, says the LORD.
Just as the heavens are higher than the earth, so are my ways higher than your
ways, and my plans than your plans.

—Isaiah 55:8-9

In consulting with many churches over the years, I have spent a lot of time focused on mission and vision. The sad truth is that too many churches have lost sight of their mission and have no clear vision for where God is calling them. Thus we end up with churches that are just going through the motions and fighting to survive.

Coaching Corner
What purpose did you identify in the last section?

Why did you choose that purpose?

A few years ago, a couple of friends and partners of mine, Dr. David Hyatt and Kay Kotan, and I wrote a workbook for churches called *Strategic Ministry Planning*. Much of that workbook was based on the works of

Aubrey Malphurs, specifically his book *Advanced Strategic Planning*. In that workbook and in our workshops we help church leaders work through the areas of values, mission, vision, goals, and objectives. In this section we are going to take a look at the areas of mission and vision as they pertain to you on an individual basis. This is your opportunity to go up a few thousand feet and look at your life from a new perspective.

Mission is typically described as what an organization does. For example, in a Christian church the mission has been given to us: "Therefore, go and make disciples of all nations, baptizing them in the name of the Father and of the Son and of the Holy Spirit, teaching them to obey everything that I've commanded you. Look, I myself will be with you every day until the end of this present age" (Matt 28:19-20).

So churches that follow Jesus should be making disciples. How about you? How would you explain to someone you just met what you do? Would your answer vary depending on the context—at work versus at church—or maybe depending on who was asking?

Don't skip over this too quickly. While this may seem a little out of place at first, how you understand what you do is critical to everything that follows. You will certainly have more than one answer—most of us do. So take a few minutes to honestly answer the question:

What is it that you do?

_____

_____

_____

How do you think others would describe what you do? Is it in agreement with what you wrote or is there a disconnect? How would your supervisor, your spouse, or your best friend describe what you do?

There are all different kinds of voices calling you to all different kinds of work, and the problem is to find out which of these is the voice of God rather than of Society, say, or the Superego, or Self-Interest.

—Frederick Buechner

How much of your time each week is actually spent doing what you just described as your mission? What would it look like (and feel like) if you were able to increase that by 10 percent? For example, what if you said that you spend twenty hours a week focused on your mission. Imagine just moving that to twenty-two hours a week. Over the course of a year that is 104 hours! A small increase each week can easily add up to some significant time over a year or more. How might that impact your mission?

Let's take a look at how a small investment now can pay big dividends later.

> He was the fifteenth of seventeen children, born the son of a poor candle-maker. He had little more than a year of formal schooling. He became an author and editor; scientist and inventor; statesman and diplomat. He was Benjamin Franklin.
>
> Benjamin Franklin was a great optimist, a visionary, a forward thinker. In his will, he left 1,000 pounds sterling each to the cities of Boston and Philadelphia.
>
> [He said,] "I wish to be useful even after my death, if possible, in forming and advancing other young men, that may be serviceable to their country in both of these towns."
>
> He specified that the money was to be used to make low-interest loans for young apprentices. One hundred years after his death, after the money had grown considerable, only part could be disbursed. It was this money that helped to create The Franklin Institute of Philadelphia and The Benjamin Franklin Institute of Technology. His additional stipulation was that the remaining money couldn't be distributed for another 100 years. In 1990, 200 years after his death, the money was worth $6.5 million. What began with a fairly small sum turned into an immense monetary amount, capable of influencing the lives of countless individuals. And it all began because of one man's small philanthropic act. (Harvey and Sedas, *The Power of 10%*)

A pastor I was coaching once shared with me that she felt very clearly that her mission was to make disciples of Christ. In between two of our coaching sessions I asked her to track how and where she was spending her time for a few weeks. During our next coaching session she shared the results and was surprised at how little of her time each week she was able to connect to her mission to make disciples. There were of course some activities, tasks, meetings, and so on that could be stretched to say they were in some way connected. But she was the one who made the final decision as to the number of hours each week associated with her mission and the total number was upsetting to her.

During a few subsequent coaching sessions we were able to identify a couple of hours each week where she could eliminate, delegate, or adjust a few items in order to focus more time on her mission. Now this is important, she did *not* adjust her schedule to work more hours. Working more hours is not really the point and not a good time-management technique. The point is to find a way to spend more of your time on what is important. This is why understanding your mission is so critical.

WORKING MORE HOURS IS NOT REALLY THE POINT AND NOT A GOOD TIME-MANAGEMENT TECHNIQUE.

Now let's look at vision. In a local church we will often say that vision is where God is calling the church to go. We will use words like, "clear and compelling" and "challenging" as we help the leaders discern God's vision. All of this should work equally well for you and your life.

As you look down the pathway of your life, where do you feel God is calling you to go? Some people have a very clear vision for their life and can share it with others even at a very young age. Many of us are able to see more of God's work in our lives when we look in the rearview mirror and not as much from the front window. How about you? Do you have a clear and compelling vision from God for the rest of your life? No? Well that is okay too. Many people are in the same boat.

Squeezing the Turnip

How have you been able to discern God's vision for your life?

"Beginning with my call to ministry, I framed each step or stage in terms of what question I believed God needed me to address at that time. Pursuing a focused question either led me to a more informed question or a different question. Having an ongoing (and developing) focused question provided me with a path to develop my work and my faith and kept me from wandering about fruitlessly."

—Gil Rendle

Let's narrow things down a bit. If you find yourself struggling too much with visualizing decades or your total life, how about visualizing the next few years? Again, don't skip through this too quickly. You may not get to hear God speaking to you in a burning bush, but you most likely have heard that still, small voice whispering in your ear. You may want to spend some time in prayer and meditation (listening more than talking) before you answer this question. That would be great.

Here are a few questions to ponder if you feel stuck before you answer the main vision question:

- What part of your job or ministry brings you the most pleasure?

- Where do you tend to see the most fruit from your efforts?

- If money were no longer an issue, what would you spend the rest of your life doing?

- Where do you tend to get the most compliments from others?

- What are you doing when time seems to fly?

- What draws other people to you?

- What do you tend to spend time teaching others?

- Where do you seem to have the most influence?

- If you could create your dream job, what would it be? What would be your job title?

Using all of this input, answer the following question as honestly and completely as possible. This will hopefully give you some direction for your personal vision.

Where do you feel God calling you in the next few years?

_____

_____

_____

Now let's pull some of this together. When we talk about mission being what we do, how does that impact time management? The obvious answer is that doing a better job of managing our time will not mean much in the long run if we are not doing what we should be doing. This is not as much about jobs or roles at work as it is about us all doing what we were put on earth to do by our creator. Before we get too deep theologically, we just need to focus a little more on our whole lives and not just on time management at work or time management in any one situation. So the mission piece is meant to keep us focused on our overall picture and not just any one part. Try thinking about it this way: how would doing a better job of managing the time God gives you each week help you be more of what God created you for?

The vision component is intended to keep us focused on where God is calling us to go and not just on the day in front of us. Many times we focus on where we want to be in a year, or two, or more. That is great. We should certainly factor that into our long-range plans and use that as part of our overall time-management process. However, let's be sure to include God in there somewhere.

The clearer we are on our mission here on earth and on our vision for the next few years, the better our opportunities to get there using the planning process we will cover in the next chapter.

Coaching Corner
Connect the dots for me between your purpose to improve your time-management skills and your mission and vision.

Optimism is the faith that leads to achievement. Nothing can be done without hope and confidence.

—Helen Keller

The way you get meaning into your life is to devote yourself to loving others, devote yourself to your community around you, and devote yourself to creating something that gives you purpose and meaning.

—Mitch Albom, *Tuesdays with Morrie*

Discussion Questions

How would you describe your personal mission?

How might your mission affect how you are spending your time each week?

What do you currently see as the vision for your life?

Discussion Questions

What steps, if any, do you need to take in order to move closer to that vision?

What excites you the most about the vision you feel God has for your life?

What scares you about this vision?

What is one small step you can take in the next thirty days toward this vision?

Most people don't aim too high and miss, they aim too low and hit.

—Bob Moawad

Prudent people see evil and hide; the simpleminded go right to it and get punished.

—Proverbs 27:12

The difference between wise people and naïve people is not what we see, but how we respond. Wise people act as if tomorrow is today.

—Mike Schreiner

Change everything, and everything will change!

—Mark Thienes and Brian Brockhoff, *Gapology*

Chapter 3

PERSONAL PLANNING

How can you best plan for your long-term, short-term, and daily activities?

I know the plans I have in mind for you, declares the LORD;
they are plans for peace, not disaster, to give you a future filled with hope.

—Jeremiah 29.11

If we do not plan our time, then our time will plan us.

The concept of planning breaks down into three main areas: long-term, short-term, and daily. We are going to take a look at each of these areas along with the overall concept of planning tools in this chapter. Let's start with long-term planning.

> ### Coaching Corner
> Hold your purpose, mission, and vision close as we go through this section.

Long-Term Planning

Long-term planning is typically more than three months out. Many churches and other organizations will concentrate on plans for a year at a time. Sometimes this is done on a school calendar or the organization's calendar, but most of the time this is done on a calendar year of January to December. When you are looking at doing some long-term planning for yourself, just pick a calendar time frame that works best for you.

In working with churches, we usually encourage them to limit their long-term planning to three to five big goals. It is best for individuals to do the same. What would you like to accomplish in the next six to twelve months?

IF WE DO NOT PLAN OUR TIME, THEN OUR TIME WILL PLAN US.

Long-term planning is very strategic in nature. At this stage we need to resist the impulse to jump into tactics and action plans. The tactics and action plans will come soon enough. But they will have a better chance of making a real difference if we invest some time and effort now in the long-term planning stage.

Most churches and people today are very busy. I've never seen a church calendar with open weeks, and I've never worked with a pastor or laity leader who is looking to fill time on their schedule. We must not confuse activity with productivity. Consider the image of a rowboat. Many leaders, and churches, are rowing like crazy but are not really sure where they are going. Long-term plans for people or organizations are like the destination we enter into a GPS. They tell us where we are going. Just like most map apps today will give us several options on how to arrive at our destination, we may find several different ways to achieve our long-term plans. Stay flexible in your methods but firm in where you are going.

WE MUST NOT CONFUSE ACTIVITY WITH PRODUCTIVITY.

Where do these long-term plans come from? How do we best discern plans for six months or more? This is where we go back to our mission and vision. What is it we really do? Where do we feel God calling us to go in our lives? Now take those very big concepts and spend some quality time figuring out what you need to accomplish in the next long-term time frame (six months or more) in order to take a step or two in the direction of that vision. In some rare cases you may feel that you will be able to actually achieve that vision God has for your life in the next year. In most cases, it will take several years or more, and this next long-term phase is more about progress than completion. Everything we cover after this hinges on the quality of our long-term plans. Without a clear picture of where we are going, managing our time well becomes pointless.

Squeezing the Turnip

How have annual (or other long-term) goals helped you in your ministry?

"I frame my semiannual goals in terms to the 'difference' I am trying to make in any area. Focusing on the different keeps me from listing a bunch of activities as if they were goals."

—Gil Rendle

As you can tell by now, long-term planning is really all about goal setting. If you were to ask a few people what their goals are they might say something like, "I want to grow as a disciple," or maybe, "I need to improve my preaching." The trouble with these types of goals is that they are so vague that you cannot do anything with them. Consequently, they are quickly forgotten.

WITHOUT A CLEAR PICTURE OF WHERE WE ARE GOING, MANAGING OUR TIME WELL BECOMES POINTLESS.

In the next chapter we are going to review a way to ensure our goals are clear and increase the likelihood of achieving the goals.

What would you like to accomplish in the next six to twelve months?

_____

_____

_____

As an example, we are going to say that you wrote this: *"In order to improve our church leadership development process, I will engage with a coach/*

consultant each month this year and implement a minimum of three new strategies so as to raise up and identify at least three new leaders by November 30."

Short-Term Planning

Your long-term plans or goals should lead you directly into your short-term plans. These plans are typically thirty to ninety days out from now. Short-term plans are still somewhat strategic in nature, but now you are starting to add in some tactical components.

YOUR LONG-TERM PLANS OR GOALS SHOULD LEAD YOU DIRECTLY INTO YOUR SHORT-TERM PLANS. THESE PLANS ARE TYPICALLY THIRTY TO NINETY DAYS OUT FROM NOW.

As you are writing these plans you should begin to see clearly the answers to the following questions:

1. What specifically has to happen?

2. Who exactly is going to be responsible for each item?

3. When is it going to be done?

4. How will it be accomplished? (What resources are required?)

The goal of short-term planning is to convert each of your long-term plans into more action-oriented steps. While it is not necessary to plan out each and every detail during this phase, it is important to begin to see "movement" toward each goal. Think about this as making your "Big Hairy Audacious Goal" (to quote Jim Collins and Jerry I. Porras in their book *Built to Last*) more bite-size.

One of the challenges that many people run into is that they try to jump directly from the long-term goals to their daily plans without spending any time on the short-term phase. This causes them to get frustrated because they are overwhelmed by the size of the goal. Investing time here by breaking your larger goals down will help you see them as more achievable and increase the likelihood of achieving each goal.

Look back now at what you wrote down on the previous page that you would like to accomplish in the next six to twelve months.

What could you do in the next thirty days to move toward that goal?

_____

_____

_____

Remember the example we shared? *"In order to improve our church leadership development process, I will engage with a coach/consultant each month this year and implement a minimum of three new strategies so as to raise up and identify at least three new leaders by November 30."*

Here are a few things you might do in the next thirty days to move toward that goal:

1. Contact three pastors you know who have used a coach in the past.

2. Research leadership coaching and consulting to find two more possible individuals to help you.

3. Set up a conversation with at least two potential coaches/ consultants.

4. Review your current leadership development process. Identify what is working and what is not.

5. Check with the largest church in your area to see what they use for leadership development. Identify one thing that will transfer to your church setting.

What else might you do in the next thirty days to move toward this overall goal?

_____

_____

_____

Before we get into daily planning, I wanted to share something I picked up from a video done by Scott Williams. In the video, called "Effectively Manage Your Time by Doing It 'God's Way,'" Pastor Williams shares that he uses a "quarterly list" of about three big items and that he ensures they are completed by the end of each quarter. In this chapter, we are focusing on connecting each level of our plans, and the quarterly list concept might have value for you as well. For example, you might take your long-term annual plans and break each of them into quarterly plans. Think about it as setting a goal each quarter to achieve 25 percent of your annual goal. Not only will this help you see the big goal as more achievable, it will also create some momentum for you as you begin to feel progress toward that overall destination.

Daily Planning

Daily planning is the phase that is familiar to most people. It can be thought of as a to-do list or as an hourly breakdown of your day. I will discuss some tips and best practices later for daily planning.

There are two keys that need to be understood now about this process:

1. You need to use some type of daily planning each day. If not, you will never reach your true productivity potential.

2. Be intentional about connecting your long-term plans and your short-term plans to your daily plans. There should be at least one item each day that has a very clear relationship *between all three*.

Daily planning is typically very tactical in nature. Setting aside an hour during your day to focus on writing your long-term goals may seem strategic, but the act of putting that on your calendar for eight thirty on Tuesday and actually doing the planning is, in reality, very tactical.

BE INTENTIONAL ABOUT CONNECTING YOUR LONG-TERM PLANS AND YOUR SHORT-TERM PLANS TO YOUR DAILY PLANS.

Take a few minutes now to create a daily plan list that would include connections to your short-term and long-term goals you wrote on the previous pages.

What is *one* action item you might do today in connection to your longer plans?

_____

_____

_____

Now look back at the long-term goal example we shared and the short-term items connected to that goal. An example of a daily item connected to those might look like this: *"9:30 a.m.—e-mail Pastor Sharron: ask whom she uses as a coach and get some feedback as to his or her effectiveness."*

Whether you use a "to-do list" or an hourly breakdown of your day, the key is to include at least one task or action item each day that is connected in some way to your overall goals. Here are a couple of things you might try as a way to improve your process of planning:

1. Keep track of your time for at least two weeks. (You may need to add more days depending on how "typical" those weeks were in your overall year.) Break it down into at least thirty-minute increments of what you are actually doing. This is just for you, so be as honest as possible.

2. Go back through each day and look for any tasks or action-type items that you could connect to a larger goal.

Squeezing the Turnip

What process do you use to plan your days?

"Personal planning is something I believe I am good at because God has given me the gift of organization. I have learned I need to have balance in all areas of my life; as a Pastoral Counselor, mother, wife and friend. I do this by starting my day with time with God. I read His Word, a devotional, other material and pray. Keeping God first and in the forefront of my day sets the pace to counsel by the direction of the Holy Spirit and to keep things running smoothly with my clients and with my family."

—Dr. Kymberly A. Hellmann, C.PhD

Throughout my years of working with leaders, I have noticed that there is usually a strong connection between those who struggle planning out their days and those who have either no goals or poor goals. We end up like the person who is taking a long car trip and finds out he or she is going in the wrong direction only to reply, "But I'm making great time!"

Most people are not able to accomplish any important goals in their life without some intentional planning. Setting great long-term goals is important; figuring out what needs to happen each thirty to ninety days for short-term plans is critical too, but daily is where the "rubber hits the road" as they say. In today's world, most leaders are busy every day and work long hours. The challenge is really more about how we are connecting those hours to our goals.

Before we leave this discussion on daily planning, let's take a quick look at the two different types of tasks.

Maintenance Tasks

Maintenance tasks are those things that we all have to do every day. They do not really move us toward a goal or necessarily help us grow, but they still have to be done. Some examples of maintenance tasks would be: eating, sleeping, driving to work, paying taxes, doing paperwork, and so on. Not that these tasks have no value, but overall they do not really add that much to our lives. But we still have to do them. What are some other maintenance tasks in your life?

_____

_____

_____

Value-Added Tasks

On the other hand, value-added tasks help us grow as a person and/or move us closer to our goals. Some examples might be: exercising, reading scripture, spending quality time with your family, planning for a vacation or retreat, working with a coach, attending a leadership development event, eating lunch with a staff person, mentoring a new leader, researching for a sermon, spending time in prayer, planning a sermon series, meeting with a local business leader, going on date night, reading a good book, spending time with God, serving in ministry, and so on.

What are some other value-added tasks in your life?

_____

_____

_____

When you do the tracking your time activity, highlight what you feel are the value-added tasks. This will give you a great visual of how you are spending your time currently. What would it look like to add one more value-added task to your life each month? What would have to go in order to make room for more value-added tasks? Again, there is no way to add more time to our days but we can always improve on how we are planning and using our time. Keep these value-added tasks in mind as you grow in the effectiveness of your time management skills. While most leaders would say that they are not intentionally adding more maintenance tasks to their lives, for some reason that is exactly what happens if we are not careful. A good sign of this is when we feel our lives getting busier and busier, but we do not seem to be getting anywhere. Value-added tasks must be added intentionally to our time while maintenance tasks just seem to show up on their own. We will talk more about value-added tasks in the Prioritizing chapter.

WHAT WOULD HAVE TO GO IN ORDER TO MAKE ROOM FOR MORE VALUE-ADDED TASKS?

Now we are going to wrap-up this section with a look at some planning tools to help us be more effective.

Planning Tools

The last part of planning I would like to discuss are tools. There are plenty of them available, and you can find them in most stores that carry office supplies, on the Internet, or in specialty stores. Many people I know, including myself, use a smart phone with apps for a calendar, notes, tasks, reminders, and other planning type options. What you use is not nearly as important as just using something that you can trust and will go to often.

My advice would be to find a tool that you feel comfortable using every day—yes, every day, and not just at work. Then customize it over time to make it your own. Look for productivity tools in the phone service you use for getting new apps. Whatever tools you end up with, ensure that they will serve at least five critical functions:

1. Calendar—For all appointments, due dates, meetings, and so on (different colors can be helpful too)

2. Organizer—For all your contact information such as phone numbers and addresses

3. Notes or Journal—For you to record information and be able to get to it quickly

4. Reminders—Sometimes built into the calendar, but a separate app can be helpful too

5. To-do list—An app of some type can be very helpful so that you can carry it with you as you go

Spend a few minutes now reviewing what you are currently using. What is working the best? Where does there seem to be a gap? What tool would help you increase your overall time-management effectiveness? Make a small investment now to add at least one new tool to your planning process. Those few dollars and the time you invest now could pay off big in the long run.

Squeezing the Turnip

What planning tool (electronic or otherwise) do you use the most?

"I've fallen in love with the online task-management tool called Wunderlist. It's intuitive, has a clean, uncluttered user interface, and allows me to organize projects in a way that makes sense for my workflow."

—Kelley Hartnett, Director of Culture and Connections at The Way

So far we have looked at strategic planning and personal planning. A main element of both areas is goals. The next chapter will focus on how to set better goals, which will enable us to become the leaders God is calling us to be. Let's look now at SMARTER Goals.

Planning is bringing the future into the present so you can do something about it now.

—Alan Lakein

Plans are nothing, planning is everything.

—Dwight D. Eisenhower

Discussion Questions

What type of long-term planning are you using now? What is working and what can be improved?

How might you transfer one of your long-term plans into a short-term plan?

What process does your church or organization use to establish long-term and short-term plans?

Who could you bring in to help with strategic planning?

Discussion Questions

What is working best for you right now with daily planning? What needs work?

What value-added task would you most like to add into your calendar next month? Why?

What planning tools and/or apps are you currently using for productivity?

Nothing is as far away as one minute ago.

—Jim Bishop

I wish I could stand on a busy street corner, hat in hand, and beg people to throw me all their wasted hours.

—Bernard Berenson

You must get involved to have an impact. No one is impressed with the won-loss record of the referee.

—John Holcomb

Don't fool yourself that important things can be put off till tomorrow; they can be put off forever, or not at all.

—Mignon McLaughlin

Chapter 4
SMARTER GOALS

How can we set better goals?

*Brothers and sisters, I myself don't think I've reached it, but I do this one thing:
I forget about the things behind me and reach out for the things ahead of me.
The goal I pursue is the prize of God's upward call in Christ Jesus.*

—Philippians 3:13-14

Coaching Corner

Did you end last year where you wanted? _____ Yes _____ No

If you could ignore all the obstacles, what would you like to
accomplish this year?

Let's recap. We started out by talking about your journey and why
you are interested in improving your time-management skills. Ensure you
keep that "why" in mind. Next, we covered the strategic planning elements
of mission and vision. What it is that you do and where do you feel God
is calling you to go? Remember that the vision element should influence
everything else. In the last chapter we reviewed the areas of long-term,
short-term, and daily planning. This chapter on SMARTER goals connects

directly to your long-term goals. We are not looking to add anything new, just to ensure that each of the long-term plans that you already identified are clear and effective by making them SMARTER.

Research suggests that churches, organizations, and people who set goals perform better than those who do not. Goals, whether personal or professional, ministry or churchwide, provide a sense of direction and meaning to our daily lives. Goals have the power to energize and motivate.

Effective goals also measure and improve performance, reduce stress, and build self-confidence. However goals that are vague, unrealistic, too challenging, or too easy can actually do more damage than good. Fortunately, there is an easy way to set productive goals.

The process can be broken down into the acronym SMARTER. Many of you may have heard of S.M.A.R.T. goals, well this is very similar—we have just added a couple of more elements. As a leader, it is important for you to be able to develop effective goals for yourself and your ministry. When you are developing goals for a ministry area or for the whole church, goal writing should be a mutual process with input from those on the team and, of course, from the staff. The concepts outlined in this chapter will work for both individuals and for groups of any size.

Before beginning the SMARTER goal writing process, it is important to separate two similar but ultimately very different terms. The terms are goals and objectives. For many, these terms are interchangeable: a goal is an objective, an objective is a goal. However, objectives should be viewed as the means to achieve goals. Activities, actions, conditions, and resources are all components of objectives. Remember the planning we talked about in the last chapter? Well, if goals are our long-term plans then objectives are our daily plans: the bullet point items that end up on our to-do list.

In my work with churches, organizations, and individuals, I have noticed two broad challenges that tend to show up at this stage. The first one is when we spend too much time in the big picture (long-term goals) and never get to the objectives. Have you seen this tendency in yourself? Do you prefer to play in the clouds and not so much down on the ground? The other challenge I've seen is when a person or group tends to go right for the objectives without really being clear on the goals. Maybe you have seen this tendency in yourself or others. As soon as there is any discussion about a big goal of some type someone goes straight to the objectives. "We should have Bill do such-and-such the fifteenth of next month." "I know Susan has experience with this, so we can contact her next week and set up a meeting." I know that these are two ends of the same spectrum and that most people are not at either extreme, but we do tend to all fall more on one side or another.

People on the big-picture side tend to think those going straight to the details are getting caught in the small stuff, and those who go right for the logistical details tend to think the others are stuck in the clouds. The truth is that we need both. But at this stage our focus needs to stay with goals until we are sure they have been done correctly. One last note on this—it is very important for us to capture some of the details that might surface during our goal-setting discussion. (We will talk more about this in a section later called Open Loops.) Write the ideas, details, comments, and so on down on a piece of paper, set it to the side, and then get back to the topic of setting the goal as soon as you can. This may be a challenge for people who love the details, but it will pay off with a better long-term plan.

While goals probably shouldn't change outright, objectives can and should be flexible and adaptable to current conditions and events. Personal, professional, ministry, or environment changes can affect the actions taken to achieve a goal.

When writing SMARTER goals, consider the actions or objectives needed to accomplish the goal and how each can be adapted to the ever-changing environment in and around our churches. Effective goals should help you achieve what you want each year and help you to keep moving forward on your journey. (They should not be a weight around your neck!)

So far we have looked at areas such as mission and vision, along with various types of planning. All of those areas should lead us to goals. But just setting a goal is not enough. We need to ensure that the goals we set will actually help us achieve what we want. When asked, most leaders would say that they know setting goals is something important and that they should be doing it. The challenge is that most of us are so busy running the race each day that we lose track of where we are going and why we are going there.

Having clear goals will not only help us, but they will help those who work with and for us. When we know exactly what our goals are, it becomes easier for us to share them with others and for them to help us achieve those goals. More on the sharing part later.

If you were to do an Internet search for "S.M.A.R.T. Goals" you would likely come up with dozens of words that can make up this acronym. (Trust me, I've done it.) They all have value and many of them are just different words to communicate the same overall meaning. For our purposes I am going to use the following:

S—Specific

M—Measurable

A—Actionable

R—Results-Oriented

T—Time-Based

E—Eternal

R—Recorded

Don't think of your goals—think from your goals.

—Unknown

As we look at each of the individual components, I would encourage you to look back at the goal you wrote down at the beginning of the previous chapter. Look for ways you can adjust what you wrote to fit the SMARTER process where needed. This will help to make each of the areas more relevant for you and increase the likelihood of remembering what we cover.

Specific

A specific goal is much more likely to be accomplished than a general goal. A key question to ask at this stage would be, "Why should this goal be accomplished?" Keep going back to ask "Why?" as often as needed to ensure you are as specific as possible. In my experience, this is the number one missing element in most goals. Individuals set goals such as, "I want to lose weight" or "Learn to speak Spanish." Churches or organizations set goals such as, "Do more local service projects" or "Reach more people." These are all nice things. But they are not specific enough. While they may be very specific in one person's head, there is real danger in trying to communicate this with others as we will see shortly.

Here is a "trick" that might help you if you are ever stuck in this stage. Try starting your goal with the phrase, "In order to _____." The words you use to fill in that blank should identify the "specific" part of your goal. This will be very important when you communicate your goal to others. Most people want to know "why" you are doing something. If the "why" is missing or not 100 percent clear, people will tend to fill in their own reasons, which may be very different than yours. Here is an example:

Let's say a church communicates out to their congregation that one of their goals for this year is to increase worship attendance by 10 percent over last year. But they do not say why. That communication gap could be filled in many different ways, most of them incorrect. People might say, "The pastor just wants more money," or they might say, "It is all about numbers in this district." Of course, those conversations always seem to take place in parking lots and hallways. Now what if the church had communicated this: "In order to live the mission Christ gave us as a church and as disciples, we are setting the goal of increasing our average worship attendance by 10 percent over last year because we want every lost sheep in our community to have a church home." Will some people still hear something different? Sure, but at least now the leaders have a clear and consistent message to share with everyone.

In their book, *Bearing Fruit: Ministry with Real Results,* Lovett H. Weems and Tom Berlin claim that the two most powerful words for fruitful leadership are "so that." I would certainly agree. The specific element of your goal is a perfect place for the "so that" to occur. "We are going to do _____ so that _____ will take place." True clarity in this element may take some thought, some time, and some prayer. Do not rush it. If the "why" or the "so that" does not automatically pop out, it usually means that there is still some level of confusion, misunderstanding, or other gray area that still needs to be addressed. Go back repeatedly to your vision. The specific element of your goal should have a very clear connection to that vision. Invest the time and energy now to be clear.

THE SPECIFIC ELEMENT OF YOUR GOAL SHOULD HAVE A VERY CLEAR CONNECTION TO YOUR VISION.

Keep in mind that simple goals are better. The easier to understand, the easier it will be to communicate and ultimately achieve them. So ensure you have a strong "specific" element to your goal before you move on to the next step.

Measurable

Can the goal be clearly measured? An effective goal will always include concrete criteria for measuring a specific result. When you are able to measure progress, you are better able to stay on track, reach your target dates, and experience the exhilaration of achievement that spurs you on to continued efforts required to reach your overall goal.

Asking "How" questions will often help you at this stage. "How many?" or "How much?" Measurable goals are quantifiable. This will most often be communicated in some type of number. This number is not the same as the goal. Numbers are just the way we will measure most goals. There may be a tendency to shy away from using numbers in some situations; this will usually result in a goal that is too vague to make any difference. Remember, if you can't measure it, you can't manage it. Many churches I've encountered have a goal to "make more disciples." That is certainly a nice idea and clearly connected to what Christ commanded us to do in Matthew 28:19-20. I also run into resistance from time to time when I challenge how the church is stating that goal. This is a good example where it might be helpful to actually move down a level or two. Here is what I mean. Are we talking about "making" more disciples? Are we focusing on growing our average worship attendance? Or are we talking about "making" those who are here already more mature disciples? Or both? Once we are clear on what we mean, then we can begin to explore what other elements might lead us to one or both of those results. For example, let's say that we are focusing on growing those who are already here more into the image of Christ. After some discussion we agree that having more of our adult congregation in Sunday school or in small groups would be a good indication of that type of growth. (Not a perfect one-to-one connection, but very few things ever are.) So we might focus on a goal directly connected to increasing the number of adults in Sunday school or small groups.

When working with churches or leaders on setting goals, I will often ask them the question, "If I come back a year from now, how will you be able to prove to me that you achieved this goal?" That usually leads us to creating a very measurable component.

Actionable

Will this goal drive you or others to actually *do* something or maybe change a behavior? Does the goal strongly suggest action of some type?

Look for strong action verbs in the goal. You should be able to clearly see in the goal that action will need to take place on your part for the goal to be achieved.

Try doing an Internet search for "action verbs for SMART goals." You may find some useful resources. The Bowling Green State University has a page on the Internet that shows a formula for developing goals: AV + A + P/D, or Action Verb + Activity + Purpose/Date. There was also a table of action verbs. Here are a few to get you started:

Achieve	Conduct	Establish	Install
Communicate	Increase	Develop	Eliminate
Formalize	Launch	Produce	Structure
Mobilize	Resolve	Teach	Unify
Prepare	Schedule	Assemble	Coordinate

Beware of some verbs that may appear to be "action verbs" but have the potential for not having much happen. Words such as *review, analyze, evaluate, identify,* and many more. If you are not careful, you might have a goal that says something like, "Evaluate the effectiveness of the Sunday school class I'm teaching about sharing personal testimonies by June 15." At first glance it looks fine. Then you "evaluate" and the answer you find is, "No one knows how to share his or her story." So you completed your goal. Was that really all you wanted to achieve? Hopefully not. This is an example where you likely needed a part two for this goal. The point here is to be on the lookout for words that can lead to misinterpretation or the creation of a goal that doesn't really move you forward.

Results-Oriented

Will this goal move you closer to your overall vision? You don't need more tasks that just create work. You need to see growth toward where God is calling you. This is always a tough area for churches and church leaders. Too often faithfulness and fruitfulness are seen as opposite ends of a spectrum, while in God's kingdom they are best viewed as a "both/and" situation.

Would reading your Bible more each day guarantee that you are growing as a disciple? No. Would someone who is growing closer to Christ on his or her spiritual journey tend to get into the word of God more often? Yes.

Does a church that is growing in attendance guarantee that they are growing disciples? No. Would a church that was effectively growing disciples each year tend to have members who were inviting new people? Yes. (They would also likely see growth in other areas such as giving, serving, missions, and witnessing, to name a few.)

It is always challenging to measure the *right* results, but we need to do our best to connect our goals and the results we are aiming at to the vision God has for our lives and for the ministry of our church.

Time-Based

Will those you share your goal with clearly see and hear completion dates? Can you write your goal down on a calendar and then break it down into smaller steps with additional milestone dates? Setting a realistic time to accomplish your goal will result in continued progress toward achievement.

Without a set time frame there is no sense of urgency.

WITHOUT A SET TIME FRAME THERE IS NO SENSE OF URGENCY.

Goals without time frames will often be pushed aside by the day-to-day time wasters that are part of most organizations. It is easy to forget about a goal when there is no deadline for completion. Meeting a deadline helps keep goals properly prioritized.

For goals with many steps or action plans, it is helpful to break down the goal into manageable stages. Work out a time frame for the accomplishment of each stage and add in time for unexpected delays. The deadline will be the date by which all stages are complete. In today's electronic world we are also able to add these dates to our calendar with appropriate reminders. This way you can use technology as a tool to help you stay on track and ensure key dates along the way so your overall goal does not get missed.

One last piece of advice on this part of setting a goal: try not to ever let a deadline pass. If you reach a point where it is no longer realistic to expect the achievement of the goal by a certain date, come up with a new date. In my experience, goals with deadlines in the past never seem to get done. We tend to see them as a failed goal. Negotiate a new deadline, with yourself or others, and then make the effort to achieve the goal by that new date.

Squeezing the Turnip

What have you learned about setting goals that you would like to pass on to others?

"Engaging in annual goal setting has been the key to doing the right things and getting results that move us forward. Even if they're not perfect, we're much better with goals than without."

—Brian Hammons, Conference Lay Leader, Missouri Conference of the United Methodist Church

---

Eternal

If completed as intended, will this goal help to advance the kingdom of God? This is intended as a check and balance to ensure our goals are focused on the right things and not just on us. Who will get the glory? This is also a good place to ensure that the goal is big enough that we cannot achieve it without God's involvement. This may not be 100 percent true of all the goals you set, but there should be at least one goal each year for you and for your church or organization that requires God's involvement to accomplish. If your vision is truly from God, God wants and expects to play a part. Review your goals. Do you have all the resources at hand to achieve all of them? If so, where are you leaving space for God? Think bigger! Push yourself in at least one of your goals so that when it is accomplished, you will know for certain that God's hand was involved. God wants to achieve great things through you and your ministry.

We may occasionally run into a personal or even a ministry goal that does not have a clear connection to advancing God's kingdom. The focus needs to be on the bigger picture. If we have four personal goals for this year and none of them seem to have an eternal element...danger! That would be a situation where we would need to go back and revisit our mission and vision and likely create at least one or two different goals.

This is also a good place to double-check our specific element: the "why" part of our goal. A church may have as its goal to install an elevator into the building. Some people, both inside and outside the church, may not immediately see how a facility item such as an elevator would have anything to do with advancing the kingdom. We know better. Jesus demonstrated many times in his ministry on earth how important it is for all people to be able to worship God. Our churches should do the same. We need for all people, regardless of their physical abilities, to have access to worship. So even when the eternal element is there in our goal, it must be clearly communicated.

Recorded

Is there a record of this goal somewhere? There should be a point of reference somewhere that you and maybe others can go back to in order to ensure clarity and understanding. Do you remember playing the "Telephone Game" as a child? Remember what happened to the message from the first person to the last? That is what happens when we do not have clearly recorded goals. Everyone has a different interpretation of the goal.

Goals that are not written down are just wishes.

—Fitzhugh Dodson

Here is a secret—if you wrote down your goals just now, you are ahead of most leaders. The vast majority of people never take the time to write out their goals. They may have some idea of where they are heading and what they want to accomplish, but they struggle sharing that vision with others. It is no wonder that they have a hard time achieving any long-term results. Congratulations on taking this important step!

One final piece of advice on goals: Do you really want to achieve them? Don't just say it. Do you really want to achieve your goals? Then share them with someone else! Accountability is born when two or more people know about a commitment. Sharing your goals with someone else and asking them to help hold you accountable to those goals will greatly increase the likelihood of you achieving them. This is one of the roles a coach can play in your life.

ACCOUNTABILITY IS BORN WHEN TWO OR MORE PEOPLE KNOW ABOUT A COMMITMENT.

004.

00000.

SMARTER Goals

Squeezing the Turnip

What would you say to a church that has never set goals before?

"To quote Dr. Phil, 'How's that workin' for you?' Without specific and measurable goals, you're left with doing what 'feels good.' And feel-good ministry rarely benefits the church, let alone the kingdom."

—Bill Tenny-Brittian, Managing Partner, 21st Century Strategies

Each day I receive the Daily Hope e-mail devotion from Pastor Rick Warren. They are always inspirational. The one below is a great companion to this chapter on SMARTER goals. After that, we will look at some ways to help prioritize everything that ends up on your plate.

Exercise Faith by Setting Goals

"An intelligent person aims at wise action, but a fool starts off in many directions" (Prov 17:24 GNT).

Once you've figured out what matters most, set goals big enough to require faith. Jesus tells us in Matthew 9 that he will bless us as much as we want. His blessing depends on the size of your faith. Jesus says, "According to your faith let it be done to you" (Matt 9:29 NIV).

You exercise faith by setting goals. What is a goal set in F.A.I.T.H.? It's:

Focused: It's specific, something you can measure.

Attainable: It's possible and practical. If you set an unrealistic goal, you won't accomplish it.

Individual: It's personal. You can't set goals for other people. You have ownership over your own goals, not someone else's.

Trackable: Your goal needs a deadline on it. Without a date on it, it's not a goal.

Heartfelt: Never set a goal you're not passionate about, because you will never accomplish it without the desire to do so. (Warren, "Exercise Faith By Setting Goals")

43

Discussion Questions

Have you ever used some type of S.M.A.R.T. goals before? If so, what has been the result?

Which element of SMARTER goals do you think will be the toughest for you?

Which element of SMARTER goals do you think will be the toughest for your church?

Discussion Questions

Name a current goal for yourself (or your church):

Identify the SMARTER elements in the above goal.

S—Specific

M—Measurable

A   Actionable

R—Results-Oriented

T—Time-Based

E—Eternal

R—Recorded

What still needs work to make this a SMARTER goal?

I learned that we can do anything, but we can't do everything . . . at least not at the same time. So think of your priorities not in terms of what activities you do, but when you do them. Timing is everything.

—Dan Millman

Action expresses priorities.

—Mahatma Gandhi

Living in light of eternity changes your priorities.

—Rick Warren

We don't drift in good directions. We discipline and prioritize ourselves there.

—Andy Stanley

Chapter 5
PRIORITIZING

How do you decide what to do first?

Don't be conformed to the patterns of this world, but be transformed by the renewing of your minds.

—Romans 12:2a

Where your treasure is, there your heart will be too.

—Luke 12:34

Coaching Corner

I'd like to affirm your progress so far. Way to go!

What has God been saying to you through the first half of this book?

Depending on where you are in your time-management skill journey, there can often be a tendency to start feeling overwhelmed by all of this. Take some deep breaths and remind yourself that this is a marathon, not a sprint. Don't give up; you have come so far already. But don't feel like you have to go from where you are today to Time Management Master all at once either. (I've been working on all this for many years and am still a long way from being a master.) The key is to make progress, take a step or two, build some momentum, and keep pressing on.

When we started this journey together we looked at why you wanted to improve your time management skills. Another way to say that might be, "Why is time management a priority for you?" God's mission for our life and for our church (Matt 28:19-20) provides a clear priority. Discerning God's vision allows us to see through all of the possible directions we might go and gives that destination a priority over everything else. We are going to continue that priority process by going even deeper.

Now that you have all those great plans (long-term, short-term, and daily) and SMARTER goals in place, how do you decide what gets done first? This is where you must make the connection between not just your daily plans and your long-term plans, but also between what you are working on each day and the goals of your church or organization—and yourself.

Mission > Vision > Goals > Objectives/Activities

This chapter will look at several different stories and ways to help you prioritize your daily/weekly activities better. Don't try to take everything and use it all in the next twenty-four hours. That will most likely make things worse instead of better. Instead, look for what really speaks to you and your style of leading. These are all great things to have in your toolbox, but it is always best to match up the correct tool to the job.

DON'T TRY TO TAKE EVERYTHING AND USE IT ALL IN THE NEXT TWENTY-FOUR HOURS. THAT WILL MOST LIKELY MAKE THINGS WORSE INSTEAD OF BETTER.

If you have developed some goals (SMARTER or not), have them in front of you as you go through the rest of this chapter. Look for ways you will be able to apply at least one of the following concepts to help you achieve those goals. If you have not yet developed goals, make yourself a note to return to this chapter once they are in place.

Priority Ranking

Here is a very practical way to prioritize your daily activities:

1. Write out your total list of what you want to accomplish today. Do not try to place them in any order or priority. Just get them down on paper.

2. Now go back and prioritize them A, B, or C. The "A" priorities must be done today. The "B" priorities need to be done soon but not necessarily today. The "C" priorities can be done any time in the near future.

3. Now add a number ranking to each of the items (A1, A2, A3...B1, B2, B3...and so on). "One" would be what you feel is the most important, "two" would be second most important, and so on within each of the A, B, and C lists. Invest a few minutes to force rank all of the items that must be done today, the ones that must be done soon, and the ones that can be done any time.

4. This is critical—*Start with A1!* Too often we start our day with something simple or easy that has no real value in the long run. "I cannot do anything until I clean up my e-mail." Or: "Before I work on my message, I need to order supplies." While this may help some people build momentum, for most of us, all it does is take time away from what we really need to be doing.

Practice prioritizing your activities for each day during a week. Figure out when you are most productive, and be sure to tackle your A1 items then. If it turns out that you seem to be most productive in the morning, then make an effort to work on your most important items then. Save the lower priority items for your less productive times. Share your list with someone to add an element of accountability if you are struggling to stay on task.

Squeezing the Turnip

What process helps you prioritize everything on your plate?

"Each week I identify all the tasks that need attention that week and then give each a score for urgency and importance. Those scores plus due dates, along with some common-sense modifications, provide the list from which daily priorities are set."

—Lovett H. Weems Jr., Professor of Church Leadership and Director of G. Douglass Lewis Center for Church Leadership, Wesley Theological Seminary

The Big Rocks

The following story can be found in many sources. I have heard it shared for years and read it in the book *First Things First* by Stephen R. Covey. You might even be able to find a video online with him demonstrating this concept. A video I saw recently on Facebook used golf balls instead of rocks. The concepts are usually the same. Here is my version:

A pastor stands up in front of the congregation and asks for a volunteer to come and help her with a demonstration. A young man jumps up and walks to the front. There is a small table next to where the pastor is standing with two one-gallon, wide-mouth Mason jars. One of the jars is empty; the other one is about three quarters full of very small pebbles. There is also a group of fist-sized rocks on the table with labels attached to them.

The pastor thanked the young man for helping out and explained to him that his assignment was to get all of the large rocks into the jar with the pebbles without going over the top of the jar. She read out loud the labels on each of the large rocks: going on vacation with family, spending time in prayer, exercising, reading scripture, working with a coach, growing your skills, grabbing lunch with a friend, reading a good book, spending time with God, serving in ministry, pursuing a new business opportunity, and having hobby time.

The young man was able to get a few of the big rocks into the jar fairly easily but then started to struggle. As he gave up on one rock the pastor read what was written on the rock and said out loud, "So you're giving up on spending time with God?" The whole church got a good laugh at that. After a few minutes the young man had only gotten about half of the rocks into the jar, and it was clear that no more would fit. He asked the pastor, "Can I use the other jar?" She said that he could.

So he put all of the big rocks into the empty jar and then proceeded to pour in all of the pebbles. It took a little effort, and he had to twist and turn the jar a few times, but eventually everything fit into the jar without going over the top.

The pastor asked the young man, "What do you think the point of this activity was?" He thought for a second and said, "If you don't put the big rocks in first, you'll never get them in at all." He was right.

Have you ever given up something really important for something that should have been a lower priority? Of course; we all have. We just need to be careful that we are not filling our days with too many small rocks. The point is that you must focus first on the most important items to you each day; otherwise, you will fill your day with small items that, in the end, do not really make a difference.

Pareto Principle (80/20 Rule)

In 1906, Vilfredo Pareto observed that 80 percent of the land in Italy was owned by 20 percent of the people—he also found that 20 percent of the pea pods in his garden contained 80 percent of the peas. This concept has come to be called the Pareto principle (80/20 rule). Many churches experience 80 percent of the work being done by 20 percent of the people and 20 percent of the congregation giving 80 percent of the offering.

Most likely the same is true for you and your ministry. You have probably seen 20 percent of your activities produce 80 percent of the fruit in your ministry. This may not be true of every day in the year but will usually show up over the weeks and months. Your first challenge: identify that 20 percent. Where are you getting the greatest return on your investment of time? The next step is to intentionally spend some extra time on those areas and try to decrease some of the time you are spending in the low-yield areas.

Remember the discussion about adding 10 percent or where you would spend an extra hour? Where you are most fruitful is a great place to make that investment. You will never be able to spend all of your time in the high-yield areas, but you can move a little more in that direction each year.

Law of forced efficiency: There is never time to do everything, but there is always time to do the most important things.

Six-by-Six

In his book *Leadership Axioms,* Bill Hybels relates the story of being on an airplane trip and trying to sort through the hundreds of challenges he had facing him when he returned home. Then he asked himself, "What is the greatest contribution I can make to Willow Creek Community Church in the next six weeks?" From that question he came up with six major items that he felt would have the greatest impact on their ministry and that he could not delegate to anyone else. Everything else he was able to either push off to later or hand off to someone else. The process seemed to work so well that at the end of the six weeks, having completed each of the six major items, he decided to do it all over again for the next six weeks.

Hybels shares that there is nothing sacred about the number of weeks or the number of items—it just seemed to work out well for him. So well, in fact, that he shared it with all of his leaders and had them start doing the same process. After a while he had all of the church leaders post their six-by-six cards, and they had quite a learning experience about what each other felt were top priorities and where they could better leverage each other for the greater good. Years later they still use this same process.

What about you? What would end up on your six-by-six list? What would happen if you shared that list with other leaders in your ministry? Try coming up with a list now just to experience the power of prioritizing your major tasks into a set time frame.

What are your top six priorities?

1. _____

2. _____

3. _____

4. _____

5. _____

6. _____

Try having everyone on your team, administrative council, ministry, and so on do the same thing, and then compare priorities. This might be very eye-opening for you to see what each other considers a top priority. Another learning experience for the group might be to see where you can help each other out with these priority items.

Squeezing the Turnip

When your schedule gets out of control, what helps you gain control again?

"When I start feeling frantic, I start making lists—or remaking them. More often than not, I've set an unnecessarily aggressive deadline, and when I take a deep breath and reprioritize, I feel liberated and can get back to work with a less frantic mindset."

—Kelley Hartnett, Director of Culture and Connection, The Way, St. Louis, MO

Eisenhower Decision Matrix

President Dwight D. Eisenhower is credited with using a simple matrix to help him make decisions and manage his time. This grid has four boxes where you can list out all of your daily activities. The story is that whenever Eisenhower was confronted with something that needed to be done he would ask himself a couple of questions: Is this task important? Is it urgent? Based on this information he would then place the task in one of four categories. Eisenhower is quoted as saying, "What is important is seldom urgent and what is urgent is seldom important." Good advice for us today.

While most of us will have some activities in each of the four boxes every day, effective time-management people have learned how to limit the items in the "not important" areas and spend more of their time in the "important" areas. As leaders, we need to work on moving more of our time out of the "not important" areas, where we are just putting out fires, and spend more of our time in the "not urgent/important" area. It is there that we will tend to see the most growth for both our ministries and us.

Try the activity for yourself. Draw out a four-by-four grid, and label it to match the Eisenhower decision matrix (or use the one below). Then list out as many of your activities from the previous week as possible. Which grids contain the most activities? Now figure out how much of your time you spent in each of the four quadrants. Are you pleased with the results? If not, what would it take for you to move just one hour a week from the other quadrants into the top right quadrant? One way to feel like you are getting blood from a turnip would be to better determine where you are spending the hours you have.

	Urgent	Not Urgent
Important	• • • • • •	• • • • • •
Not Important	• • • • •	• • • • •

ONE WAY TO FEEL LIKE YOU ARE GETTING BLOOD FROM A TURNIP WOULD BE TO BETTER DETERMINE WHERE YOU ARE SPENDING THE HOURS YOU HAVE.

Pastor Rick Warren spoke of this same concept in his Daily Hope devotional called "Focus on the Important, Not the Urgent."

"Make the most of every opportunity in these evil days" (Eph 5:16 NLT).
I've got good news and bad news for 2014. The 365 days you'll be given next year aren't enough time to do everything. But here's the good news: God doesn't expect you to do everything. God has given you just enough time to do everything He wants you to do.

That's why it's so important for you to set goals for 2014. Goals help you focus your life. Paul models this in 1 Corinthians 9. He says, "I do not run without a goal. I fight like a boxer who is hitting something—not just the air" (1 Cor 9:26 NCV). Paul had a purpose. You need one too.

Too many of us focus our lives on unimportant causes. Trivial Pursuit isn't just a game; it's a description of our culture. Most of what's going on in our world today won't matter in a week—much less for eternity.

Most people can't tell the difference between urgent and important. Urgent is almost never what's important. We set aside family time, our time with God, and our friendships for the urgent matters that almost never matter for long.

Goals are a great antidote for the kind of life that chases the urgent rather than what's important. Goals will focus your energy. (Warren, "Focus on the Important, Not the Urgent")

That is great advice for all of us as we reflect back on what was covered in this chapter. The main topics covered were: priority ranking, the big rocks, the Pareto principle, six-by-six, and finally the Eisenhower decision matrix. Hopefully each of these gave you some ideas you will now be able to incorporate into your planning process as you prioritize what is really important. Just be careful to only focus on adding one thing at a time.

One final thought on prioritizing your activities. As we've already covered, at least some of your daily/weekly action items or objectives should be clearly connected to your larger goals. Take one of your goals and break it down into as many small objectives as you feel are appropriate. (A good rule of thumb here is that each objective should take no more than fifteen to thirty minutes to complete.) Now schedule each of those objectives on your calendar. Don't try and do too many on any given day, but ensure that they all find a home somewhere in your week, month, or year. This activity will help you to see each objective as a task to complete and not just as a bullet point under your goals. This will also allow you to see if any of your objectives are too large and need to be broken down into smaller parts if they will not fit onto your calendar. The best part of doing all this should be your ability to now see the larger goal as something that can be achieved when broken down into smaller parts and the visual of incorporating these objectives right into your calendar. If all this is still a little too much to grasp at this point, here is a smaller step that might help. Take your to-do list for a day or a week. Now place each item on your calendar as appropriate for the day or week. Doing this is a form of force ranking your items and should help you see how incorporating each of your goal's objectives will work. The bottom line is that most of us tend to accomplish more when things are actually on our calendars and not just on a list of things we want to do someday.

Discussion Questions

Which one of these stories will you use to improve your ability to prioritize your schedule? Why?

What are the "big rocks" in your life? Do they always get first place?

Where are you spending most of your time currently on the Eisenhower decision matrix?

What would it take for you to move more items into the not urgent/ important quadrant?

Reality check. If you are a pastor reading this, you might be thinking this right about now: "This is all great, but I don't control a lot of what gets put on my schedule." This is true. There may be no other profession like a pastor of a local church where a person's calendar is controlled so much by others.

If this is true for you, instead of throwing up your hands, what can you actually do to make some small steps in the other direction?

Do you control your schedule or does it control you?

What can you do to take back more control of your schedule?

_____

_____

_____

Every pastor and ministry leader I've worked with has at least some interest in becoming more productive with their time. Now that we have a good foundation in place with our goals and know how to prioritize our activities, it is time to review a few ways each of us can increase our productivity.

Don't be a time manager, be a priority manager. Cut your major goals into bite-sized pieces. Each small priority or requirement on the way to ultimate goal becomes a mini goal in itself.

—Denis Waitley

Concentrate all your thoughts on the tasks at hand. The sun's rays do not burn until brought to a focus.

—Alexander Graham Bell

It is better to strike a straight blow with a crooked stick than spend my whole life trying to straighten the darn thing out.

—Ken Blanchard

If you want to make an easy job seem mighty hard, just keep putting off doing it.

—Olin Miller

Chapter 6
PRODUCTIVITY

What are some ways you can make better use of your time?

Laziness brings poverty; hard work makes one rich.

—Proverbs 10:4

But examine everything carefully and hang on to what is good.

—1 Thessalonians 5:21

Coaching Corner
On a scale of one to ten, with ten being the best, how would you rank your average daily productivity?

What tends to get you off track from being as productive as you want?

When are you most productive?

Are you most productive first thing in the morning? After lunch? In the late afternoon? Take a minute to identify when you think you are at your very best on most days. Now consider what types of tasks or activities you tend to do during those times. Are you working on important but not urgent type activities (from Eisenhower's Decision matrix) or are you doing things that are not really that important in the long run...like e-mail? What would happen if you were able to match up your peak performance times with your top priority items? While that might not be realistic for every day during the year, imagine the impact this would have on your goals if you could do it just once or twice more a month. The key here is learning to be intentional.

Everyone can improve on how productive we are with our time each day. Please don't mistake productivity with working harder or having the most items on your to-do list crossed off. The important thing here is that you are working toward your goals and getting there on time or ahead of schedule. I love the quote from John Wooden: "Don't mistake activity for achievement." How many times have we seen someone who is working very hard but never seems to get much done? As an example, I will often take time during the day to read an article, watch a video, read a book, or maybe research some information on the Internet. It may look to others that I am not being very productive at those times, but I am actually working on my goals to learn more and grow myself as a leader.

I LOVE THE QUOTE FROM JOHN WOODEN: "DON'T MISTAKE ACTIVITY FOR ACHIEVEMENT."

We are going to look at six different, but related, areas in this chapter:

1. Best Practices—These are tips and tricks that I have picked up over the years from books, training seminars, or other sources to help increase productivity. Look for one or two that you can begin to put in place soon to help increase your productivity.

2. Time Wasters—These are things that tend to suck away at our overall productivity. Most likely we have all experienced at least a few of these over the years. Make plans now to remove, or at least reduce, these in the near future.

3. Stop/Start/Continue—This is an activity that leaders should do occasionally to ensure we are focused on the right things.

4. Multitasking—This is a myth that we will talk more about shortly.

5. Open Loops—We will look at what these are and some ways to close them in order to make us more productive.

6. Vacation—Not during...but before.

Best Practices

The following are some best practices that I've picked up over the years. *Don't try to add all of them at once!* Look for one or two that speak the most to you in this season of your ministry. Use a new best practice for at least thirty days in a row in order to make it a habit.

- Plan your day's total activities, not just your work. Your personal life often overlaps with your work and vice versa. Your calendar, planner, or other tools should be complete and not compartmentalized.

- Write it down! (On paper or electronically.) More on this shortly.

- Learn to say "no" when needed. Adding on more does not work for long. Sometimes we need to decline even what looks like a good opportunity.

- Get enough sleep. Most of us need at least seven to eight hours of quality sleep each night. Listen to what your body is telling you.

- Put your goals in front of you. Keep them posted somewhere you can see them each day. Check to ensure that at least some of what you are doing each day is connected to those goals.

PUT YOUR GOALS IN FRONT OF YOU. KEEP THEM POSTED SOMEWHERE YOU CAN SEE THEM EACH DAY.

- Establish a set time each day to do some planning. Maybe it is the first few minutes when you get to work each day to plan that day. Or maybe it is the last part of your day before you go home to plan the next day. Either way, invest some time to plan before you jump into the day.

• Plan for the unexpected. It will happen anyway, so you might as well build it into your schedule. A good rule of thumb is to have at least thirty minutes in the first half of the day and another thirty minutes in the last half of the day.

• Break large tasks down into smaller action steps. If it is going to take you more than fifteen minutes to complete a task, it can most likely be broken down. Doing smaller tasks creates momentum and will help a big task seem smaller.

• Find someone to hold you accountable. I mentioned this before, but it is worth repeating. It can be your spouse or a partner at work (or both). Share your plans with them and ask them to challenge you periodically on your progress.

• Delegate and coach. Take something off your list every day, and delegate it to others. If you cannot do so, then it is time to coach, train, and develop someone right away so you will be able to delegate soon.

• Recognize procrastination when it happens. Find ways to break out of the traps (see Time Wasters).

• Enjoy what you are doing. I don't think Marc Anthony said it first: "If you do what you love, you'll never work a day in your life."

• Start your day the night before. Put items needed for work in the car at night. Start writing your to-do list.

• Never leave a meeting without an action plan. Who is going to do what and by when? If there is no action plan, then the meeting may have been a waste.

• Imagine you are paying everyone at the meeting one hundred dollars or more an hour, including yourself. Are the problems you are dealing with worth that investment? Too often we are spending thousands solving hundred dollar problems.

- Don't serve food at a meeting unless absolutely necessary. It will add time to every meeting.

- Touch it only once. This used to apply mostly to papers crossing our desk. Today much of what we deal with is electronic. But we still tend to read the same e-mails over and over again or keep too many windows open at once with stuff we will get to later. Eliminate some of your distractions by "touching" it only once.

- Set an offbeat meeting time. People will more likely remember a meeting with a time of 6:47 than they would a 7:00 meeting. Most people allow extra time (we usually don't get going until 7:10) when the meeting time is on the half hour. Be sure to start on time!

- Check out the most popular productivity apps every few months. See if there is something new that will help you.

- Arrange your office so that you don't face the door. People are less likely to interrupt if they cannot see your face.

- Try setting a time limit for certain tasks instead of working from start to finish. Works best with large tasks where you may need a break or two.

- If it is going to take less than five minutes to complete, do it now! Don't put it off.

- Plan for waiting times. We all face them. Doctor's office, airport, and so on. Make sure you have something with you that will add value and not just fill the time.

- Set specific times during the day for e-mail and social media. Don't let them run your day. Just because you get an e-mail every few minutes or there is a new posting every second does not mean you have to stop everything else to read them as they arrive.

- Go deeper. Take a class on time management. Read some books on the subject.

- Hire a coach to partner with you and help hold you accountable.

- Ask someone. Look around and find someone who seems to be a little ahead of you in the area of productivity. Ask them to share with you what works best for them and incorporate what you can.

Time Wasters

- Phone calls / e-mail / Internet / social media—Whatever happened to technology freeing up our time? Today it seems like we lose more and more of our time each year to these "tools" and the latest tech toys. One key for each is to set boundaries. For example, only check e-mail three times a day for thirty minutes each.

  o Phone calls—Let your voicemail answer a call if you are working on a top priority item. Try standing up when you take a call to help speed up the conversation. Schedule times to talk instead of doing calls "on the fly." (I once had an executive tell me, "Phone calls are only convenient for the person placing the call.")

  o E-mail—Ask to be removed from mailing lists that do not add value. Handle each e-mail only once—read and then file, respond, or delete. Don't use e-mail as "chat"—pick up the phone or text. Use a tool such as color codes or something similar to indicate high priority people so you can better sort you list.

  o Internet (or intranet)—Clearly define what you are looking for before you start searching at random. Stay away from sites that are more entertaining than informative.

  o Social Media—Even when used for "work" purposes these can become huge time suckers. Limit your activity where you can and avoid just checking to see what everyone else is doing until you are off work.

- E-mail, part two—Here are a couple of other items to look out for with e-mails: When a string of e-mails gets too long (multiple replies and/or forwards), it is usually best to start a whole new e-mail. We end up wasting a lot of time reading all of the connected responses. A related item is the subject line. Too often the topic within the body of the e-mail no longer matches the subject line. Even if you are not going to start a whole new e-mail, it would save everyone time to update the subject line.

- Ineffective or unnecessary meeting—We have all been in a meeting where we felt like it was a complete waste by the end. What did you do about it? Ensure there is a clear agenda where possible; look for ways to communicate information without a formal meeting; always start and end on time. (Read the book, *Death by Meeting* by Patrick M. Lencioni for more great tips about how to make meetings more productive.)

- Socializing—The key is to balance between connecting with people and getting your work done. Be aware of those who socialize too much, and limit your interaction with them where possible.

- Disorganization—Contrary to popular belief, a cluttered desk is not a sign of a genius; it is a sign of someone wasting time looking for what they need.

- Procrastination—This is one that almost everyone struggles with in one way or another. Try breaking down large projects into smaller pieces that can be done each day to avoid waiting until the last minute. Watch out for "deadline high" where you seem to get energy doing everything just before it is due—this may actually feel good at the time, but it will cost you and those around you in the long run.

Squeezing the Turnip

Is there a time waster that you have learned to overcome?

"This one is embarrassingly simple. I travel frequently and find airplane-time to be some of my most productive time. Why? Because (until recently at least) I am totally disconnected from all streams of communication. No e-mail, no Internet, no phone. When in the office, needing to focus on writing, Bible study, planning, or some other intense activity, I close the e-mail client, web browser, and turn off the phone. Creating a space devoid of potential interruption."

—Rusty Lewis, Vice President of Generis

- Interruptions/unexpected visitors—Create a signal for your team so they know when they can and cannot interrupt you. Establish a set time each day when you are available for questions or direction. Stand up when someone enters your work area; it will help both of you to get to the point and get back to work. (I know a pastor who does counseling and has what he calls "thirty-minute chairs" in his office. They are only comfortable for about thirty minutes so people tend to not overstay their time.)

- Micromanaging—Understand your team well enough to know who needs more direction/feedback and who does not. Agree to time frames for follow-up when tasks are assigned, and stick to them. Invest time in training and developing others, and that will pay you back in major dividends later.

Those are, of course, just a few of the top time wasters. Did you recognize any that you are struggling with now? Don't worry—everyone struggles with at least a few of them from time to time.

Here are a few key points to help with time wasters in general:

1. Work on moving from reactive to proactive. We all fight fires from time to time. Once the fire is out it is important to take the time to learn what caused the fire in the first place. Learn to prevent more fires than you put out.

LEARN TO PREVENT MORE FIRES THAN YOU PUT OUT.

2. Make smart investments of time each day that will save you time in the long run. For example:

   a. Check for clarity in your communications to ensure understanding and prevent having to communicate over and over again.

   b. Train/coach those you work with first to get them up to the expected level so that you can begin to delegate more often.

   c. Take a break when you need it. Find some ways to recharge your batteries. Know when your peak times are and when they are not.

Stop/Start/Continue

This is an activity I was introduced to early on my leadership journey. I was on a team with some other trainers, and our company was growing very quickly, so the training department had to reevaluate everything we were currently doing and clearly identify where we needed to go in the next few years. We went to a conference room and put three flip charts at the front. On the first one we wrote "stop," on the middle one "start," and on the last one "continue."

On the "stop" flip chart we listed out all of the items that we were currently doing that we felt either did not fit with the company direction or that we would no longer have the resources to do. We were very intentional about trying to match the anticipated resources from the "start" items to the "stop" items. Our department did not plan to grow by much, so we knew that we would need to stop doing at least one item for everything new we started.

On the "start" flip chart we listed out everything we could come up with that we were not currently doing but felt that we would need to start doing soon in order to support where the company was heading. Interestingly, I recall very clearly that one of those items was leadership development.

On the "continue" flip chart we listed out everything that we were currently doing that we felt must continue. As we discussed each of these items, it was clear that most of them would see some type of change or adjustment very soon, but we also knew that they were generally needed to support the organization.

This type of activity also works for churches, individuals, or any other group or organization. I've never worked with a church of any size that wasn't busy. Every church calendar is full. That great idea you have for a new ministry—that big new goal that is going to move you closer to your vision—requires resources. Chances are that the people you have in mind to serve on that new team are already involved somewhere else. (The very best people in most organizations are not sitting on the sidelines waiting to be called.) For you to start something new, it will likely require stopping something else.

As you look at your month, quarter, or year, what are the main areas where you spend time or resources? Now take that list and put it into the three categories: stop, start, and continue.

What are you doing now that either no longer supports your ministry or the fruit produced does not match your investment so you need to *stop*? (This may still have value but needs to be handed off to someone else.)

What are you not currently doing that you will need to *start* doing soon in order to better support your ministry?

What are you doing that must *continue*?

Set aside some time at least once a year to complete this activity for yourself and with the ministry team or group that you lead. Be sure to surround this process with prayer. Focus on discerning—what is God calling you to stop, start, and continue?

Multitasking

Multitasking is a myth. God did not wire us to be able to do more than one thing at a time. We may think that we are doing multiple things at once, but what we are really doing is constantly switching back and forth between activities. Each time we switch we lose focus and productivity. There are, of course, times where we need to work on more than one item, but we need to realize that we are decreasing our overall effectiveness. (This has been shown in several studies over the years. Yes, for both men and women.)

MULTITASKING IS A MYTH. GOD DID NOT WIRE US TO BE ABLE TO DO MORE THAN ONE THING AT A TIME.

Think of a time when you felt like you were effectively multitasking. Most likely you were using technology or some other type of tool to do one task while you were working on the other. Now think back to a time when you might have gotten yourself in trouble by trying to multitask (while driving?). You were probably focusing more on one task than the other, which is perfectly normal for most people.

While our world today practically demands that we are doing multiple things at the same time, remember that we are usually sacrificing at least some attention and productivity when this happens. Whenever possible try putting 100 percent of yourself into one task at a time. Get it done then move on to the next. You will find yourself saving time in the long run.

The same people who brag about being able to multitask often then complain about not being able to focus fully on anything (family, work, God, and so on).

Open Loops

Have you ever been reading your Bible and suddenly thought of a chore or task you needed to do? (Pick up laundry, go to the grocery store, send an e-mail, write a newsletter article, and so on.) How about this—have you ever had the same "reminder" pop into your head multiple times during the day? Most of us have experienced this more than a few times.

In his book, *Getting Things Done*, David Allen refers to this as an "open loop" and emphasizes the need to close these loops in order for us to increase our productivity. He refers to this challenge as incomplete commitments we have made with ourselves. They can be large commitments such as "plan out the next six months of message series," or smaller commitments such as "write a thank-you note to ladies who provided food for our meeting."

Imagine your mind as a large lake. Your peak productivity is achieved when the lake is calm and clear. All of these incomplete commitments are like buoys that occasionally float up to the surface. Not only do they reach the surface, they also cause ripples. You can push them back down, but they are still under the water, waiting to rise up again and interrupt whatever it is that you are doing at the time (and the timing is usually very inconvenient).

IMAGINE YOUR MIND AS A LARGE LAKE. YOUR PEAK PRODUCTIVITY IS ACHIEVED WHEN THE LAKE IS CALM AND CLEAR.

There are three things you can do to close some of these loops and thus increase your overall productivity:

1. Stop what you are doing (even reading scripture), and record what reached the surface of your mind.

2. Clarify the commitment. What exactly do you need to do?

3. Put the reminder that you recorded somewhere that your mind will know it will be seen later by you.

4. Just do it! Don't put it off if it is something you can do right now.

Let's use the example listed above concerning the thank-you note that you need to send to the women who provided a meal for the meeting last night. This incomplete commitment has been bouncing around in your mind ever since you thought of it during the meeting. This open loop is preventing you from concentrating fully on anything else. So you grab a sticky note and write "thank-you notes" on it. Will this close the loop? Maybe. But it could also cause more ripples. What if you look at this note later and think it was a reminder to buy more thank-you notes and you cannot recall why you needed more? The point here is that the clearer you are, the better your chance of really closing the loop. It is a lot like having someone's name pop up on a calendar reminder. "Is he calling me or was I going to call him? What is his number? Maybe he was coming by my office . . . I hope I was not supposed to meet him somewhere!"

Vacation

No, I'm not talking about being productive while you are on vacation. Think about the last time you went on a vacation for a week or more. Now remember the day before you left to go on that vacation. If you are like most leaders, that was a very productive day. You had to make quick decisions about all of your open items and about everything that came across your desk that day. Having a clear deadline in front of you most likely caused you to deal with it, delegate it, trash it, or put it off to another time.

Sorry, we cannot add to your vacation time. However, there are some very good learnings from that experience.

- What are you handling more than once that would save you time if you just dealt with it now?

- What items on your list this week could be delegated to someone else? Why are you doing it anyway? Many leaders like to hang on to certain things that they enjoy doing even when they are low priority and could be done by someone else.

- Are there items that you are dealing with multiple times that should just be ignored or trashed? The next time you delete some e-mails or throw away some paper, consider how many times you read it first.

- It is okay to put some things off till later. The key is to still give them a deadline and to get them off your desk and your mind until then.

We have now looked at six different but related areas concerning productivity: best practices, time wasters, stop/start/continue, multitasking, open loops, and vacation. Which one spoke the most to you at this stage in your life? Be careful trying to add too much of this all at once. The results could be exactly opposite of what you were trying to achieve.

I Just Don't Have Enough Time!

A master coach, J. Val Hastings, shared the following in a post recently:

A common complaint I hear from leaders is "I don't have time to get everything done."

A simple strategy that often helps is to divide your to-do list into two categories:

Solid-time activities

Split-time activities

Solid-time activities require larger blocks of *uninterrupted* time. Split-time activities are those items that can be accomplished rather quickly, and interruptions and distractions have little impact, if any.

The next steps are simple:

1. **Schedule blocks of time to accomplish the solid-time activities.** Consider going off site. Tell others not to interrupt you. Gather everything you will need for the solid-time activity ahead of time so that you are ready to begin your work at the designated time.

2. **When you have a free moment, or are in-between events, work on your split-time activities.** Keep this list current and readily available.

I've been using the solid-time and split-time strategy for years, and I'm amazed at how much more productive I am. (Hastings, "I Just Don't Have Enough Time!")

Time is free, but it's priceless. You can't own it, but you can use it.
You can't keep it, but you can spend it. Once you've lost it,
you can never get it back.

—Harvey MacKay

Discussion Questions

What are you going to use from this chapter first? Why? When?

What best practice are you planning to try?

Which of the time wasters hit closest to home? What are you going to do about it?

Discussion Questions

Where might you use the stop/start/continue concept?

When are you most productive? When are you the least productive?

What are you planning to do next in order to improve your productivity? When are you going to start?

Productivity is never an accident. It is always the result of a commitment to excellence, intelligent planning, and focused effort.

—Paul J. Meyer

Time is the only coin of your life. It is the only coin you have, and only you can determine how it will be spent.

—Carl Sandburg

Unlike other resources, time cannot be bought or sold, borrowed or stolen, stocked up or saved, manufactured, reproduced, or modified. All we can do is make use of it. And whether we used it or not, it nevertheless slips away.

—Jean-Louis Servan-Schreiber

Sometimes I get the feeling that the two biggest problems in America today are making ends meet and making meetings end.

—Robert Orben

Chapter 7
NEW HABITS

What do you want to echo from your life?

The one who claims to remain in him ought to live in the same way he lived.

—1 John 2:6

Remember that your character is the sum total of your habits.

—Rick Warren

Coaching Corner

Have you already started to progress in an area that you would like to continue?

Reward yourself! Do something positive that will reinforce that progress and keep you going.

Don't give up.

Never, never, never give up.

—Winston Churchill

It takes about twenty-one days of doing something every day for it to become a habit. That means that if you truly want to improve some aspect of your time-management skills, you will need to focus on it each and every day for at least three weeks just to give yourself a chance. That is a lot. But it can be done.

Think about when you learned another skill such as how to speak a new language or how to play an instrument. Very few people can pick up a guitar and play it or read a book on ancient Hebrew and start translating Bible text. Improving your time-management skills requires practice and patience.

I once taught a class on time management for a major retailer, and we had a section on habit-forming tips. Here are a few of those tips:

- Start small—If you want to make a big change, sometimes the best thing to do is to take small steps to get there. Let's say you want to form the habit of exercising for thirty minutes each morning. A small start might be to get up thirty minutes earlier than usual and exercise for ten minutes. Do that for a week or so, and then add five minutes of more exercise each week. Consider rewarding yourself along the way. These small incentives can help build momentum.

IF YOU WANT TO MAKE A BIG CHANGE, SOMETIMES THE BEST THING TO DO IS TO TAKE SMALL STEPS TO GET THERE.

- Have variety—Do not confuse forming a new habit with doing the exact same thing over and over again every day. There is power in changing things up every once in a while. Think about wanting to form the new habit of returning all phone messages within twenty-four hours. Try doing that at different times during the day: when you first get in, after lunch, or before you leave. This change in your behavior will help break the routine and produce different outcomes.

- Connect with your goals—There is a greater chance of success if you can clearly see and feel a connection between your new habit and at least one of your major goals. A colleague of mine once had the goal of getting a college degree. She had to develop the habit of setting aside at least an hour a day to study and complete her class work, even when she was traveling. It was easier for her to establish this habit because she could clearly see the connection with her long-term goal. She kept her goal in front of her by posting it where she would see it each day and tracked her progress each week on her calendar.

- Replace the old with the new—Do not spend time and energy focusing on getting rid of a bad habit. It is a better investment to focus on the replacement habit. If you want to stop the habit of writing your sermon at the last minute, try starting the new habit of breaking your message prep into small pieces you can do each day. It takes ninety days or more to break a bad habit but only twenty-one days to establish a new habit. You pick. Avoid the trap of abandoning your new habit when you mess up the first time. This happens to us all. Practice forgiving yourself, and get back to the new habit as soon as possible. If you find yourself struggling too much with establishing a new habit, that may be sign that you have "bitten off more than you can chew" and need to start with something smaller and work your way back up to where you were going.

IT TAKES NINETY DAYS OR MORE TO BREAK A BAD HABIT BUT ONLY TWENTY-ONE DAYS TO ESTABLISH A NEW HABIT. YOU PICK.

Back in 2010, my pastor, Mike Schreiner, did a sermon series called Echo about how we could all better echo the life of Jesus. One of the weeks was titled, "His Habits: My Habits," and I thought some of those main points might be good reminders for us in our discussion on habits.

Habits determine the outcome of our lives. As Jesus moved through life, he was constantly pressured to go off course. He stayed on track with his purpose by employing habits that countered the opposing forces against him. We, too, can begin developing and maintaining constructive habits that can lead us to successful living.

1. The Habit of Solitude

"But Jesus would withdraw to deserted places for prayer" (Luke 5:16).

What do you think was the benefit of solitude for Jesus? What changes in your life routine would you need to make to allow time for solitude?

2. The Habit of Bible Study and Application

"Every scripture is inspired by God and is useful to teaching, for showing mistakes, for correcting, and for training character" (2 Tim 3:16).

Read for depth not distance. Jesus developed the habit of understanding and applying scripture in his life. He used scripture to respond to and overcome Satan's temptations. How can you develop this habit of understanding and applying the word of God in your life?

READ FOR DEPTH NOT DISTANCE.

3. The Habit of Prayer

"Jesus was telling them a parable about their need to pray continuously and not to be discouraged" (Luke 18:1).

"What if you woke up tomorrow and the only things you had were those that you had thanked God for today?"

Where is your prayer life the strongest, and where do you need to focus?

4. The Habit of Community

"He appointed twelve and called them apostles. He appointed them to be with him..." (Mark 3:14).

Jesus spent three years of his life modeling for his followers the importance of community. When we rely on our own perspective in life, we often slip into convenient rationalizations and blind spots. We need people who invest in our lives—people who share authenticity with us and who are truth tellers.

What habit of Jesus do you need to work on in this season of your life and ministry?

Squeezing the Turnip

What has helped you develop the habit of Bible study and application?

"I have a longstanding personal practice: I absolutely do not leave the house each day until I have looked reflectively with God at scripture and have received from God a 'word' for that day to carry with me. Some days it is literally a word—like *respect*, or *finish*, or *prepare*—to provide a few examples. Throughout the day I repeat the word as the prayer of my heart in each circumstance or situation, and it guides me to listen and to look for the leading of the Spirit. This daily practice has unfailingly helped me stay on course with time, energy, focus, and mission."

—Sue Nilson Kibbey

"When there's no vision, the people get out of control..." (Prov 29:18). Vision is discerned from solitude where the noise of the world falls away and God's voice is most clearly heard. Solitude is not an option—it is essential for leaders in the church. Communion with God is like an annual performance review when discernment, wisdom, vision, and therefore enthusiasm and joy are all renewed. Two to five days of solitude annually are essential for the leader who truly leads."

—Ken McDonald, Regional Director Alpha USA and Planting Pastor, Lighthouse Community Church, Lake St. Louis, MO

A few final thoughts on habits. In the book *Outliers: The Story of Success,* Malcolm Gladwell mentions the "10,000-hour rule" where he claims that it takes at least 10,000 hours of practice to master a skill. This is different than what we are referring to in this chapter when we talk about habits. In the area of time management, when we refer to habits we are really looking at those small things that can help us manage our time better and are done out of routine. While it is true that most habits take time to develop, we should be able to establish them in a lot less than 10,000 hours. The Chinese proverb, "The best time to plant a tree was twenty years ago. The second best time is now," is a very good guide for us to use when we look to develop new habits. We may wish that we were more organized or better at planning our days or weeks. We may also wish that we had started working on these habits years ago. It is never too late! While we cannot go back and start a positive habit twenty years ago, we can start it today. I am reminded of something from the C. S. Lewis book *Mere Christianity* that I will paraphrase here for our discussion on habits. Imagine you are walking through the woods along a path with a couple of other people. You come to a fork in the road and all of you go to the left. After a while it becomes clear to all of you that you have taken a wrong turn and you should have gone to the right at the fork in the road. (This is where I would say to my wife, "We may be lost, but we're making great time!") The first person in the group to turn back is going to be the first one to reach the correct destination. You may have a habit that you wish to start, a habit you wish to break, or a habit you wish to strengthen. The sooner you start working on it, the sooner you will reach your goal.

Before we look at margin, take some time by yourself or with your class or group to answer the questions on the following pages. One of the best ways to establish or grow a habit is to share it with others who can encourage you and hold you accountable. This is also a great role for a coach.

Patience and perseverance have a magical effect before which difficulties disappear and obstacles vanish.

—John Quincy Adams

Discussion Questions

What are you going to use from this chapter? Why?

Is there a habit you would like to break?

What new habit would you like to establish?

What are you going to actually do in order to establish this new habit? (Remember, it is best to start small.)

Where Do You Need Some Margin?

    Use the chart below to indicate how full you feel each of the areas are currently in your life.

    The fuller you feel an area is, the more you should shade in that section.

    In this context we are not saying "full" in the good sense, but in the sense that you have no available space for anything else in that area.

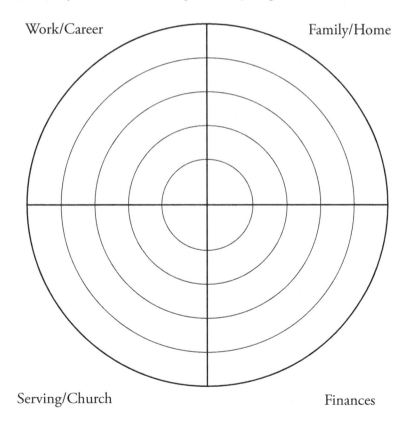

Work/Career

Family/Home

Serving/Church

Finances

Chapter 8
MARGIN

Is there space between your load and your limit?

The thief enters only to steal, kill, and destroy. I came so that they could have life—indeed, so that they could live life to the fullest.

—John 10:10

Coaching Corner
What brings you closer to God?

How are you intentionally creating space for God to speak into your life?

Filled up lives limit the full and abundant life Jesus offers.
Which is easier to read?

RemembertheSabbath-daybykeepingitholy.Sixda-ysyoushalllaboranddoallyo urwork,buttheseventhdayi saSabbathtotheLORDyour-God.Exodus20:8-10aNIV	Remember the Sabbath day by keeping it holy. Six days you shall labor and do all your work, but the seventh day is a Sabbath to the LORD your God. —Exodus 20:8-10a NIV

Both sides are exactly the same, except the one on the right has space between the words and around the sides. God wants us to have margin in our lives. All of us were created with limits.

"If our days are fixed, the number of our months with you, you set a statute and we can't exceed it" (Job 14:5).

When our margin shrinks, our stress goes up. Have you ever experienced this in your ministry? Too often we lead filled up lives with increased stress and decreased productivity. Why do we keep filling up our time and our lives? It usually boils down to two main areas—we are afraid of missing out and/or we are afraid of falling behind. A preacher was once asked why he never took a day off. His reply was, "The devil never takes a day off!" I think he had the wrong role model for his ministry.

Some leaders struggle with a "need to be needed." Maybe it is insecurity, maybe it is ego, but whatever the reason they need to feel like everyone needs them for everything. Nothing happens in their ministry unless they are directly involved. They may not have any margin in their lives but when they go to bed at night it is a "good tired." This is not a good model for others and is rarely sustainable for long.

Jesus's life had a distinct pattern: **engage** and **escape**.

"Right then, Jesus made the disciples get into the boat and go ahead to the other side of the lake while he dismissed the crowds. When he sent them away, he went up onto a mountain by himself to pray. Evening came and he was alone" (Matt 14:22-23).

Your life moves to a better place when you move at a sustainable pace. God tends to speak to us in the margins. God wants us to lead a life of margin. It is important for us as leaders to remember that others are looking to us as an example. We need to take care that we are not saying one thing and doing another.

"Come to me, all you who are struggling hard and carrying heavy loads, and I will give you rest. Put on my yoke, and learn from me. I'm gentle and humble. And you will find rest for yourselves. My yoke is easy to bear, and my burden is light" (Matt 11:28-30).

Margin requires faith.

Margin produces peace.

Margin produces possibility.

Why talk about margin in a book about time management? Because they are very closely connected. As I hope you have seen so far, effective time management is not about filling our days with the most stuff. We tend to be more productive and focused when there is margin in our lives. Just like God intended. A key component to margin is taking at least one day a week to both worship and rest.

Sabbath is God's space between the activities of life.

Sabbath: To cease from work.

God created time. Have you ever stopped to think about that? Everything we use to base our concept of time (the sun, the moon, and so on) was created by God. Without Genesis 1, we would not have our days, weeks, months, or years.

God limits our time. As we read in Job 14:5, we each only have a certain number of days on this planet. The good news is that this world is not our home; we are aliens here. Some of us get many years and some only a short while. But there is nothing we can do to change the limit God has set.

God created the Sabbath. God prescribes the Sabbath.

"On the sixth day God completed all the work that he had done, and on the seventh day God rested from all the work that he had done. God blessed the seventh day and made it holy, because on it God rested from all the work of creation" (Gen 2:2-3).

"Remember the Sabbath day and treat it as holy. Six days you may work and do all your tasks, but the seventh day is a Sabbath to the LORD your God. Do not do any work on it—not you, your sons or daughters, your male or female servants, your animals, or the immigrant who is living with you" (Exod 20:8-10).

Jesus took one day off a week—is your mission more important than his?

JESUS TOOK ONE DAY OFF A WEEK—IS YOUR MISSION MORE IMPORTANT THAN HIS?

Sabbath is a blessing from God.

"The Sabbath was created for humans; humans weren't created for the Sabbath" (Mark 2:27).

Sabbath is a witness to our faith.

"The LORD said to Moses, 'Tell the Israelites: "Be sure to keep my sabbaths, because the Sabbath is a sign between me and you in every generation so you will know that I am the LORD who makes you holy"'" (Exod 31:12-13).

Sabbath creates time for God to work for me.

"On the sixth day the people collected twice as much food as usual, two omers per person. All the chiefs of the community came and told Moses. He said to them, 'This is what the LORD has said, "Tomorrow is a day of rest, a holy Sabbath to the LORD. Bake what you want to bake and boil what you want to boil. But you can set aside and keep all the leftovers until the next morning"'" (Exod 16:22-23).

God's Promise

If you stop trampling the Sabbath, stop doing whatever you want on my holy day, and consider the Sabbath a delight, sacred to the LORD, honored, and honor it instead of doing things your way, seeking what you want and doing business as usual, then you will take delight in the LORD. I will let you ride on the heights of the earth; I will sustain you with the heritage of your ancestor Jacob. The mouth of the LORD has spoken. (Isa 58:13-14)

Let's end this chapter by focusing on some practical applications. The whole concept of margin can seem a little tough for many people to get their heads around. Don't let that discourage you from finding the margin God wants you to have in your life. First, identify the areas of your life were you feel that you currently have margin. Even a small amount should be celebrated. Be sure to protect those areas as you move forward. Next, determine *one* area where you would like to have more margin (with your spouse, with your family, alone time with God, hobby time, mentoring a young leader, and so on). Identify a small step in that area that you feel will increase your margin. Set a date for when you will take that step. Share it with someone else—especially the other person if they are involved. Take that step! After an appropriate amount of time, evaluate the results. If you did not increase your margin, try again with a different step. If you did increase your margin, celebrate and plan step two. Third, identify someone whom you feel is a good example of having margin in his or her life. Set up a time with him or her to ask a few key questions and gain insight into how he or she goes about gaining and protecting margin.

Parts of this chapter were based on a message series called Margin and some of the accompanying materials from Pastor Mike Schreiner of Morning Star Church.

Finish each day and be done with it. You have done what you could. Some blunders and absurdities have crept in; forget them as soon as you can. Tomorrow is a new day. You shall begin it serenely and with too high a spirit to be encumbered with your old nonsense.

—Ralph Waldo Emerson

Discussion Questions

Where do you need more margin in your life?

What specifically are you going to do next to gain more margin in your life?

What is God saying to you about the Sabbath?

Who is a good role model for margin? When are you going to talk with him or her?

Seven days without rest makes one weak.

—Ben Patterson

However beautiful the strategy, you should occasionally look at the results.

—Winston Churchill

There is a difference between interest and commitment. When you're interested in doing something, you do it only when it's convenient. When you're committed to something, you accept no excuses; only results.

—Ken Blanchard

I am the true vine, and my Father is the vineyard keeper. He removes any of my branches that don't produce fruit, and he trims any branch that produces fruit so that it will produce even more fruit. You are already trimmed because of the word I have spoken to you. Remain in me, and I will remain in you. A branch can't produce fruit by itself, but must remain in the vine. Likewise, you can't produce fruit unless you remain in me.

—John 15:1-4

Chapter 9

FRUIT

What do you want to produce?

A good tree can't produce bad fruit. And a rotten tree can't produce good fruit.

—Matthew 7:18

Sorry, I lied. It's not all about you.

As Christian leaders, we all know better. It is not really all about us. As we read in 1 Peter 2:9-10, we are all called into the ministry. Some are ordained into full-time ministry. The rest of us may have other positions, but we are still ministers.

Let's review what we covered throughout this book:

- Foreword—Pastor Mike shared with us the differences between chronos and kairos time. As Christians, we live in both and need to be good stewards of the time God has given us.

- Introduction—We learned that we cannot get blood from a turnip—only God can give us more time, but we might be able to squeeze out some more time by learning to be more productive and efficient.

- The Journey—We identified why better time management was important for us and identified our personal purpose for growing this skill.

- Strategic Planning—We focused on our personal mission (what we do) and vision (where God is calling us to go).

- Personal Planning—We covered the concepts of long-term, short-term, and daily planning along with planning tools. We also looked at the differences between maintenance and value-added tasks.

- SMARTER Goals—We learned how to set more effective goals that are specific, measurable, actionable, results-oriented, time-based, eternal, and recorded. These are our long-term plans which tie directly back to our vision.

- Prioritizing—We looked at the areas of priority ranking, the big rocks, the Pareto principle, six-by-six, and the Eisenhower decision matrix and focused on picking one that speaks directly to you.

- Productivity—We covered the six different but related areas of best practices, time wasters, stop/start/continue, multitasking, open loops, and vacation. Don't try to add all of them at once! Pick one or two that will work best in this season of your ministry.

- New Habits—We learned some important ways to form new habits along with the habits of Jesus: the habit of solitude and the habit of Bible study and application.

- Margin—We emphasized the importance of having space between our load and our limit like Jesus showed us in his ministry pattern of engage and escape.

Squeezing the Turnip

How do the results in your ministry connect back to your investment in setting goals?

"Every six months I list all the projects on which I'm working and, for each, ask a series of questions. One of the most important of those questions is, 'Of all these things, which ones will make the most difference for the church fifteen years from now?'"

—Lovett H. Weems Jr., Professor of Church Leadership and Director of G. Douglass Lewis Center for Church Leadership, Wesley Theological Seminary

"'If you fail to plan, you plan to fail' is a cliché because it's true. When I make plans and execute plans, the results always outweigh the inconvenience of having to take time to pause, to pray, to ponder, and to plan."

—Bill Tenny-Brittian, Managing Partner, 21th Century Strategies

---

Throughout Jesus's ministry and the books of the New Testament, we encounter a focus on producing fruit from our lives and our ministry. How about you? What fruit do you want to be able to show from your ministry?

Look back at the beginning of the book to see what you wrote concerning why time management was important to you. That should give you a good clue as to where you desire to see some fruit. Then review the other chapters to see what really spoke to you personally.

As you look down the path of your journey as a Christian leader, what are the results (fruit) that you would most like to see from your ministry?

Discussion Questions

What fruit do you want to see in your ministry?

Next week God is going to give all of us another 168 hours. What are you going to do with yours?

Don't lower your expectations to meet your performance. Raise your level of performance to meet your expectations. Expect the best of yourself, and then do what is necessary to make it a reality.

—Ralph Marston

Direction—not intention—determines your destination.

—Andy Stanley, *The Principle of the Path*

Time flies. But you are the pilot.

—Scott Williams

The difference between the impossible and the possible lies in a person's determination.

—Tommy Lasorda

The dictionary is the only place that success comes before work. Work is the key to success, and hard work can help you accomplish anything.

—Vince Lombardi

Servants, do what you're told by your earthly masters. And don't just do the minimum that will get you by. Do your best. Work from the heart for your real Master, for God, confident that you'll get paid in full when you come into your inheritance. Keep in mind always that the ultimate Master you're serving is Christ. The sullen servant who does shoddy work will be held responsible. Being a follower of Jesus doesn't cover up bad work.

—Colossians 3:22-25, *The Message*

Chapter 10

KEY LEARNINGS AND NEXT STEPS

What will you do now?

Focus your eyes straight ahead; keep your gaze on what is in front of you.... Don't deviate a bit to the right or the left; turn your feet away from evil.

—Proverbs 4.25, 27

Key Learnings—What were the top things that you picked up from reading this book?

_____

_____

_____

_____

_____

_____

_____

Key Learnings

_____

_____

_____

_____

_____

_____

_____

_____

_____

_____

_____

_____

_____

Next Steps—What are the next two or three small steps you will take in order to put in place what you have learned?

_____

_____

_____

_____

Who can you get to hold you accountable?

_____

(one of the roles a coach could play in your life)

Time is nothing more than a gift from God, and we must be good stewards of it. When it comes down to it for me, time management is just the biggest component of self-management. It's what Oswald Chambers called, 'absolute total surrender.' God owns it all—our time included.

—Steve White, consultant and author, *Please Change Your Mind*

You may delay, but time will not.

—Benjamin Franklin

Don't say you don't have enough time. You have exactly the same number of hours per day that were given to Helen Keller, Pasteur, Michelangelo, Mother Teresa, Leonardo da Vinci, Thomas Jefferson, and Albert Einstein.

—H. Jackson Brown Jr.

A Final Word

I enjoy hearing pastor Rob Bell speak and love the videos he has done with NOOMA. In August of 2003, he spoke at Willow Creek Community Church, and his message is called "Between the Trees." I found a copy of the video on the Internet and loved the way he was able to connect the way we look at our time here on earth with what God gave us in his word. Pastor Bell described how Genesis opens with a scene of the tree of life and Revelation closes on the same scene. So here we are living our lives between the trees.

> Then GOD planted a garden in Eden, in the east. He put the Man he had just made in it. GOD made all kinds of trees grow from the ground, trees beautiful to look at and good to eat. The **Tree-of-Life** was in the middle of the garden, also the Tree-of-Knowledge-of-Good-and-Evil. (Gen 2:9 *The Message*, emphasis added)

> Then the Angel showed me Water-of-Life River, crystal bright. It flowed from the Throne of God and the Lamb, right down the middle of the street. The **Tree-of-Life** was planted on each side of the River, producing twelve kinds of fruit, a ripe fruit each month. (Rev 22:1-2 *The Message*, emphasis added)

I also like how Pastor Bell points out that in Genesis 2:15 it says, "GOD took the Man and set him down in the Garden of Eden to work the ground and keep it in order" (*The Message*). Not sure about you, but I always had this image of Adam and Eve just taking it easy until they got kicked out of the Garden. Turns out they were working. Doing meaningful work. Not working their fingers to the bone but also not just lounging around. I like the image of God giving them work to do. And I believe God has given us meaningful work to do, too. My prayer for you is a life full of righteousness, wisdom, and good work.

The fruit of the righteous is a tree of life, and the wise gather lives.

—Proverbs 11:30

BIBLIOGRAPHY

Albom, Mitch. *The Time Keeper.* New York: Hyperion, 2012.

Allan, David. *Getting Things Done: The Art of Stress-Free Productivity.* New York: Penguin Books, 2001.

Belkin, Lisa. "HuffPost Poll: What Would You Do With An Extra Hour Every Day?" *The Huffington Post,* August 2, 2013. http://www.huffingtonpost .com/2013/08/02/extra-hour-a-day_n_3697387.html.

Bell, Rob. "Between the Trees." Video. Willow Creek Community Church, August 27, 2003. http://youtu.be/eDF9qS7mvrE.

Bennis, Warren C., and Burt Nanus. *Leaders: Strategies for Taking Charge.* 2nd ed. New York: HarperCollins, 2003.

Bowling Green State University. "Action Verbs for SMART GOALS." https:// www.bgsu.edu/content/dam/BGSU/human-resources/documents/training /i9-tools/action-verbs.pdf.

Collins, Jim, and Jerry I. Porras. *Built to Last: Successful Habits of Visionary Companies.* 3rd ed. New York: HarperCollins, 2002.

Cottrell, David, and Mark Layton. *175 Ways to Get More Done In Less Time.* Dallas: CornerStone Leadership Institute, 2003.

Covey, Stephen R. *The 7 Habits of Highly Effective People: Powerful Lessons in Personal Change.* New York: Simon & Schuster, 1989.

Covey, Stephen R., A. Roger Merril, and Rebecca R. Merrill. *First Things First.* New York: Simon & Schuster, 1994.

Dittmer, Robert A. *151 Quick Ideas to Manage Your Time.* Franklin Lakes: The Career Press, Inc., 2006.

Duncan, Todd. *Time Traps: Proven Strategies for Swamped Salespeople.* Nashville: Thomas Nelson, 2004.

Gladwell, Malcolm. *Outliers: The Story of Success.* New York: Little Brown and Company, 2008.

Hastings, J. Val (Founder and President). "I Just Don't Have Enough Time!" Blog. Coaching4Clergy, April 22, 2014. http://coaching4clergy.com/i-just-dont -have-enough-time/.

Harvey, Eric, and Michelle Sedas. *The Power of 10%: How Small Changes Can Make a BIG Difference.* Flower Mound, TX: Walk The Talk, 2008.

Hybels, Bill. *Leadership Axioms: Powerful Leadership Proverbs.* Grand Rapids: Zondervan, 2008.

Lencioni, Patrick M. *Death by Meeting: A Leadership Fable...About Solving the Most Painful Problem in Business.* San Francisco: Jossey-Bass, 2004.

Lewis, C. S. *Mere Christianity.* New York: Macmillian, 1952.

Malphurs, Aubrey. *Advanced Strategic Planning: A New Model for Church and Ministry Leaders.* Grand Rapids: Baker Books, 2008.

Maxey, Cindi, and Kevin E. O'Connor. *10 Steps to Successful Time Management.* Alexandria: ASTD Press, 2010.

Schreiner, Mike. "10.29.13." Morning Star Church video blog, October 29, 2013. vimeo.com/78102855.

Steve Miller Band. "Fly Like an Eagle." *Fly Like an Eagle* (album). Capitol Records. 1976.

Tracy, Brian. *Eat That Frog!: 21 Great Ways to Stop Procrastinating and Get More Done in Less Time.* San Francisco: Berrett-Koehler Publishers, Inc., 2001.

Warren, Rick. "Focus on the Important, Not the Urgent." Daily Hope Devotional, January 6, 2014 (e-mail). http://rickwarren.org/devotional/english/focus -on-the-important-not-the-urgent.

Warren, Rick. "Exercise Faith By Setting Goals." Daily Hope Devotional, January 5, 2014 (e-mail). http://rickwarren.org/devotional/english/exercise-faith-by -setting-goals.

Warren, Rick. *The Purpose Driven Life: What on Earth Am I Here For?* Grand Rapids: Zondervan, 2002.

Weems Jr., Lovett H., and Tom Berlin. *Bearing Fruit: Ministry with Real Results.* Nashville: Abingdon Press, 2011.

Williams, Scott. "Effectively Manage Your Time by Doing It 'God's Way.'" Nxt-LevelSolutions.com video, October 5, 2011. http://www.churchleaders .com/outreach-missions/outreach-missions-videos/156418-how-to-manage -your-time-god-s-way.html.

ABOUT THE AUTHOR

Ken Willard is the owner of Leadership4Transformation, LLC. He lives in St. Louis, Missouri, with his wife, Mary, where they attend Morning Star Church.

Ken is a Christian Leadership Coach focused on meeting leaders where they are and helping them take the next steps on their leadership journey. He is an ACC level coach with the International Coach Federation, a member of the faculty with Coaching4Clergy, a coach trainer, and has over 400 hours coaching pastors and laity leaders since 2009.

Ken is also a certified church consultant with the Society for Church Consulting. He has lead church consultations all over the country with all types and sizes of churches.

Ken has written and developed many leadership courses for both pastors and laity leaders in use today by churches and conferences all over the country. He also has over fifty courses available online at www.Leadership4Transformation.com. He facilitates live workshops with churches and larger groups on topics such as strategic ministry planning, evangelism, discipleship, connections, coaching, leadership development, time management and many more.

You can reach Ken via e-mail at: Ken@L4T.org to find out more about having him work with you, your church, district, conference, or other group.

Equipping God's People to Expand God's Kingdom!

LEADERSHIP**4**TRANSFORMATION

Our Mission Is to
Equip God's People 4 Transformation

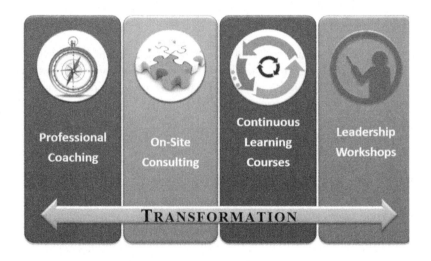

Ken Willard
ken@L4T.org
www.Leadership4Transformation.com

CPSIA information can be obtained at www.ICGtesting.com
Printed in the USA
LVOW04s2257250315

432009LV00001B/1/P